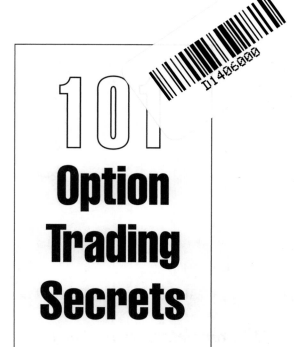

101
Option
Trading
Secrets

Also by Kenneth R. Trester

The Complete Option Player
The Option Player's Advanced Guidebook
Secrets to Stock Option Success

101
Option
Trading
Secrets

KENNETH R. TRESTER

Institute for Options Research, Inc.
Lake Tahoe, Nevada

Option Master® is a registered trademark of the Institute for Options Research, Inc.

Leaps® is a registered trademark of the Chicago Board Options Exchange

Cover Design by Brad Greene, Greene Design
Illustrations by Tim Sheppard, Olivia Trester and Robert Turner
Text Design by Sans Serif

Trester, Kenneth R.
    101 Option Trading Secrets/Kenneth R. Trester
    Includes index
    ISBN: 0-9604914-4-9

    1.Options (Finance) 2. Options (Finance)-Computer network resources. 3.Internet (Computer network) I. Title. II. Title: 101 Option Trading Secrets

Published by:
Institute for Options Research Inc.
P.O. Box 6629
Lake Tahoe, NV 89449
www.optionbooks.com

2nd printing - December 2004

To Olivia

*Her editorial and artistic talent
helped make this book a reality.*

SECRETS

Section 1: Preparing to Play

Section 2: The Prediction Game

Section 3: Option Buying

Section 4: Option Writing

Section 5: Option Analysis

Section 6: Spreading

Section 7: Trading Tactics

Section 8: Trading Tips

Section 9: Trading Resources

Section 10: Power Plays

Section 11: Tutorial

INTRODUCTION

Option trading is one of the greatest games on earth! You can be a two-dollar investor, betting on the action of stocks, the markets, futures and/or commodities, or you can be the casino or a legalized bookie, taking the bets instead of making the bets. You pick the role and have the fun and profit. With options, gains of over 1000% are not unusual, and you can design strategies that will win up to 90% of the time.

Better yet, options are an excellent investment tool that gives you much more flexibility, reduces your risks and increases your income in the investment markets. Once properly learning to use options, you will use this tool in your investment portfolio for the rest of your life.

However, many novice option traders, as they start trading, encounter many disappointments and issues in the options markets and leave with a bitter taste, for they have unrealistic expectations and are not equipped to compete in this game. This book will help the novice option traders as well as the experienced option traders become better equipped to stay in the game and compete successfully.

I have been trading options since the option exchanges first opened in 1973 and have seen *everything*. As an option newsletter writer starting in 1973, I have monitored and talked to hundreds of traders. Now you can have the benefit of all this experience and information. This book provides important nuggets of knowledge about option trading that I have collected over the past thirty years: strategies, tactics and methods that have worked and not worked for me and my subscribers.

Some secrets are classics or old adages heard on Wall Street for many decades, but that do work. Others use the new technologies that are available today. Some secrets are common sense. Others are quite unique. Many will help you avoid paying a high tuition as you learn to trade options or try to improve your skills.

If you are a beginner, make sure to read the tutorial at the end of this book. If you need further education, read my book, *The Complete Option Player*, now in its 4th edition, which makes options very easy to understand.

Then prepare to have revealed to you a lifetime of option trading secrets. Just a few of these nuggets could make the difference between winning and losing the option game.

Section 1

Preparing to Play

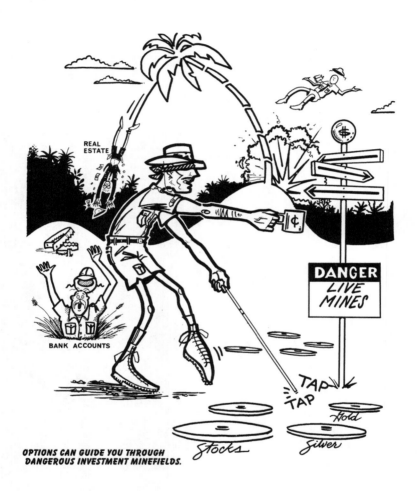

OPTIONS CAN GUIDE YOU THROUGH
DANGEROUS INVESTMENT MINEFIELDS.

1

THE SECRET ADVANTAGES OF OPTION TRADING

Option trading has been considered by many to be speculative and dangerous, and the buying of stock, in comparison, to be conservative and safe. Despite these views, the bear market of 2000–2002 saw the Nasdaq dive in value, with many high flying stocks dropping 90% in value.

Truly, buying stocks in the 90's bull market was like walking through a minefield blindfolded. If you owned the wrong stocks and you were caught in the bear market downdraft, your portfolio would have been in devastating danger.

Here lies the secret advantage of trading options. If you

would have owned options instead, you could have greatly limited your losses. The big advantage of options is that you have outstanding leverage, but (and here is the key) with limited risk.You can only lose what you pay for the options, and that can be a small amount.

Therefore, instead of owning high flying tech internet stocks that have a dramatic amount of downside risk, you could receive the same kind of leverage by buying options and utilizing option strategies yet only risking 10% of your portfolio.

The advantage of option trading does not stop there. Options provide a way to buy stocks at lower prices and, while you're waiting for the stocks to drop to lower prices, make money. Options provide a way to earn additional income from your portfolio, and options enable you to buy an insurance policy on your stock portfolio that is not available from any insurance company.

With options you can design investment strategies that will profit regardless of what the market does. Besides, you can design these strategies with extremely attractive risk-reward pictures, much better than any other investments. Furthermore, options enable you to design strategies that will win over 90% of the time.

For speculators, options provide the opportunity for spectacular gains. Gains of 1000% are not that difficult to attain. Over the years from 1982 to 1999 that I wrote the option advisory letter, *The Trester Complete Option Report*, the overall theoretical performance of our option buying recommendations showed over 1500% return in two of the seventeen years.

One of our recommendations showed a 10,000% gain. Even

during the bear market of 2000–2002, there was an opportunity for great success. For example, I bought call options on Philip Morris (MO) at 2.5 ($250), one of my few option purchases for the year 2000, that rose to 27 ($2700). This was almost a 1000% return.

Moreover, options enable the speculator to become a casino, where you take the bets instead of make the bets. Here you can truly make a living as an option trader.

Options are an extremely valuable risk-reduction, profit-maximizer tool. In fact, for all investors, options are an extremely valuable tool and can be used with all of your investment activities.

But, like all miracle drugs, options must be used with prudence and proper care, for if you overdose, options can be dangerous to your financial health.

2 EDUCATION, EDUCATION, EDUCATION

To be a successful option trader, you must get the proper education. Without the education, you can, indeed, walk through a minefield. Reading this book is a good start. If you are unclear about options, make sure to read the tutorial at the back of this book or *The Complete Option Player*, a very easy-to-understand, but comprehensive coverage of option trading. Try to read everything you can on options by the option authorities who are also active traders, such as Larry MacMillan's, *Options As a Strategic Investment*.

Take a course on options. There are video and DVD courses available if you can't get to a classroom setting. The value of these courses and books is that just one nugget of knowledge taken from these courses can greatly improve your performance in the market.

Again, try to stay with the option authorities that trade actively and that don't fill their presentations with hype! Getting an education may seem time-consuming and expensive, but ignorance can cause far more pain and expense.

Secret

3

PLAY IT
ON PAPER

If you are a beginner to option trading, getting started can be a difficult task. One way to gain the confidence to trade options is to play it on paper first. Let's call it exhibition season or preseason games where you get to make errors without losing any money. Make some theoretical purchases of options and play as if you have real money in the game.

Playing it on paper becomes more important when you are considering high risk trades, such as naked writing. Then you want to be fully comfortable with the strategy and be sure of the pitfalls before you put some real money on the line.

Once investors put real money in the game, their behavior changes. RISK and GREED come into play, and the greatest enemy of all, the ego, gets in the way.

When you paper trade, you will act rationally, but once

investors really trade, they tend to become irrational. One of the greatest battles of option traders is to maintain their rationality.

When you paper trade, nothing is at risk, so it is like walking a straight line across your living room. However, when you have money at stake, it is like walking on a ledge of a twenty story building. Suddenly it is a lot more difficult walking a straight line because fear comes into play.

Therefore, don't paper trade for too long, for real learning only occurs when real money is on the line; you will pay a tuition in the real world even if you paper trade for a long time.

4 STICK A TOE IN THE WATER

During the seventeen years that I wrote *The Complete Option Report* newsletter, I found that many of our subscribers never traded an option. Although I don't have hard statistics, my guess is that 50% to 70% read the report and left it on the cocktail table. Why? They could not build up the nerve to trade.

The beauty of options is that you can play and risk very little. Options can cost as little as $5.00 (the cost of a cocktail) to control 100 shares of stock. And when you buy options, the most you can lose is what you pay for the option, nothing more.

Consequently, buying options is the best way to start trading options. Avoid entering spreads or option writing. Just buy a small number of options to get your feet wet. If it's only going to cost you the price of eating dinner out, why not give it a try. Also, as you read this book, you will discover some hidden secret strategies to buying options.

The key is to break the ice, and even if buying only a few cheap options is not economical from a commission standpoint, at least you get in the game.

Though you might be planning on entering far more risky or complex trades, such as spreads or option writing, I suggest, to gain experience, that you start by taking some very small positions. Again, only stick one toe in the water. Then if you make some mistakes, you will not pay a high tuition for your experience. Here you're still in preseason, but you have some of your real money on the line, which provides for a much more meaningful learning experience.

Overall, no matter how good the situation may look, avoid plunging into the water!

Secret

5

DO YOUR HOMEWORK

"The will to win is important, but the will to prepare is vital."

—Joe Paterno

When I taught option trading courses at the college level, I would break the class into groups. Each group would manage a theoretical options portfolio. The performance of their portfolio would determine their grade for the class. At the end of the semester, I surveyed the class to determine how much time each group spent meeting and managing their portfolio. The result was quite revealing. There was a high correlation between time spent managing the portfolio and the performance results. The best performing groups always spent the most time managing their portfolio.

Hence, make sure to do your homework before you invest.

With options, that means doing option analysis before entering an option strategy and then properly monitoring that position.

I once asked a successful trial lawyer, who was a good friend, "What is your secret to success?" He said that when he entered the courtroom, he had always done his homework, but most opposing attorneys had not done their homework and weren't prepared.

Before you enter the options markets, do your homework, and you will separate yourself from the crowd.

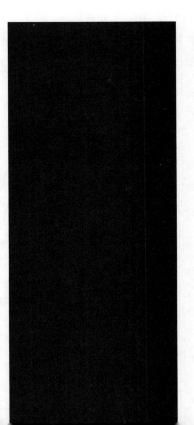

Section 2
The Prediction Game

THOSE WHO USE CRYSTAL BALLS
EAT CHIPPED GLASS

Secret

6

THOSE WHO USE CRYSTAL BALLS EAT CHIPPED GLASS

"It is not for us to forecast the future but to shape it."
— Antoine de Saint-Exupery

Every one tries to beat the market by trying to predict the future. The problem is that 90% of all investors are horrible failures at trying to predict short term moves in stocks, indexes and futures. Even the professional shows a dismal record.

Study after study shows that 80% to 90% of the stock mutual funds underperform the indexes and stock market averages year after year. This means that investing in an Index Fund where no management is involved is wiser than investing in a mutual fund of stocks. There is no need to pay those management fees.

This also tells you that future stock price actions are unpredictable. When the pros, who are paid hefty salaries, can't beat the averages, who can?`

In fact, the brokerage firms spend millions and millions of dollars trying to find systems that will predict future stock and commodity prices, and their results have not been good. Some of our top scientists spent millions of dollars trying to develop a system for predicting stock prices and were unsuccessful. (However, they were able, after extensive research and testing, to develop a system to predict index prices. Check out the book, *The Predictors* by Thomas A. Bass.)

Hence, there are no crystal balls for predicting the markets. Academic studies strongly suggest that the markets move randomly (Check out *A Random Walk Down Wall Street* by Burton G. Malkiel, now in its 8th edition.) And, if the top brains and specialists, backed by millions of dollars, can't beat or predict stock movements, why should you be able to do so? Therefore, the best way to approach the markets is to assume that they are random.

Many investors that I have encountered have a totally irrational view of their ability to predict the market. On numerous occasions, investors have asserted that they were 99% sure that the market would move up or down, and most of the time they have been wrong. In fact, some have become angry when I say that the markets approach randomness.

The problem that all investors face is that the markets are very efficient. That means that they have digested and discounted all the information that is available and, thus, have discounted present trends and potential future events.

Furthermore, in this information age of the internet, this discounting occurs very rapidly. For example, the stock market moves six months before events occur, such as a recession bottom. Consequently, almost all future price moves are based on surprise news and events not available to the public.

As for trend followers, trends can be changed radically by *chaos theory* , which states that small unrelated events can have a major impact on future events or trends. Therefore, it is best to assume the markets are random, rather than try to predict and bet on the unpredictable.

The big advantage to options is that you don't need a crystal ball. In fact, you don't have to be right about the market 50% of the time. Some option strategies win 90% of the time regardless of what the market does. If you are an option buyer, one winner can pay for many losses. As a result, you can be wrong about the market most of the time and still be a winner.

In my *Complete Option Report*, when making recommendations over seventeen years, I assumed that the markets were random. We always recommended three puts and three calls for purchase in each issue. Even with this random approach, the options theoretical portfolio showed impressive returns over that period.

So, throw out your crystal ball and trade options!

BEWARE OF LADY LUCK!

Secret

7 BEWARE OF LADY LUCK

Most investors invest by the seat of their pants, and when they are successful, they believe they can predict the markets. In many cases, it is a matter of pure luck.

When you buy options, your odds of winning on any play are lower than most people think. My *Complete Option Report* track record in the 80's showed two years with an overall percentage return of over 1500%, but only 20% of the positions recommended were profitable. Your probability of winning when you buy options will always be less than 50% in a random market. Furthermore, with out-of-the-money options, that percentage can drop dramatically.

Here it is important to understand your odds of winning. Millions of people buy lottery tickets, yet your chances of winning the big prizes are so remote that you have the same chance of winning whether you play or don't play. State lotteries are actually a voluntary tax system. Knowingly or not, people who play are making a voluntary tax payment to their state.

In the casinos of Nevada, there is an ancient game of Keno where twenty numbers are picked from one to eighty. Fifteen-point Keno, where you try to pick fifteen out of twenty numbers, pays $100,000 for a $1.00 ticket. What are your odds of winning? Your true odds are over 430 billion to one. Of course, no one has ever hit the fifteen-spot Keno, and they never will, but thousands of gamblers keep trying.

Throughout the book, we will emphasize how to measure your odds of winning when you trade options. However, even if you know your odds of profiting, Lady Luck will try to trick you, for in the world of probabilities, there are winning streaks and losing streaks.

Here is an example: during the 2001 National Basketball League (NBA) playoffs, the Sacramento Kings in one game missed twenty-two 3 point shots at the basket in a row, and they were one of the highest scoring teams in the league. Now a NBA player should hit a 3 point shot about 35%–40% of the time, so even if your odds of winning approaches 50%, you still can have long losing streaks. Therefore, even if you are doing everything right when you trade options, you could incur a long losing streak.

Such streaks discourage the option trader. Many quit or change their system or methodology and start making the wrong moves, extending their losing streaks. We see this behavior frequently with baseball players. When they go into a slump and cannot get a hit, they change their style of hitting and slip into a greater slump.

Lady Luck has a tendency to make us look very brilliant or very stupid. Consequently, as you trade options, beware of Lady Luck. If you are an option buyer, be prepared for losing streaks, stick to your game plan and don't get discouraged.

Of course, this is difficult to do and is a major obstacle for the option buyer. If you can't handle a lot of losses, then you might want to consider option strategies with much higher probabilities of profit, which we will disclose in future chapters.

To reiterate, as you trade, beware of Lady Luck and don't let her trick you into making the wrong move!

8 REGRESSION BACK TO THE MEAN

"Regression back to the mean" is a statistical law that indicates that when the results for some specific period or series of events is extremely good or extremely bad, you can expect the results to move closer to normal or the long term average.

For example, if a baseball team is really hot and wins a lot of games in a row, it is likely to win fewer games in the future. In pro football, the super bowl champion is likely to show poorer performances in the next year, especially at the beginning of the season, as it regresses back to the mean.

The same applies to the stock market. A hot fund manager is likely to cool off next year. A wild bull market is likely to end up in a bear market or major correction. When the stock market is very quiet, it is likely to get much more volatility—the calm before the storm. Options that are cheap and undervalued are likely to become properly valued or expensive, and overvalued options tend to get less expensive.

The regression back to the mean phenomenon is quite obvious when investors pick mutual funds or investment advisors. Generally, investors have very short vision. They only look at present performance when much of that performance could be luck rather than skill. Here you are likely to see regression back to the mean. Today's hot mutual funds are likely to underperform in the future.

The law also applies to your behavior. If you are on a hot streak, look out! You're due for a losing streak as you regress to the mean.

"Regression back to the mean" is one of the few tools that you can use to forecast the future.

9 BEWARE OF GURUS

Many option investors are always in search of a free ride. They are looking for the guru that will lead them to the promised land or the system that is the Holy Grail. There is no system that will work all the time, and although there are analysts who are very good, they, too, will have their cold streaks.

One well known advisor once predicted market moves eleven times in a row and then suddenly and over a three year period missed several major moves in the market. This is an example of why picking a truly good advisor can be quite difficult. Good performance is usually the result of Lady Luck, and if the markets are unpredictable, a guru in the long run will not provide much help.

Nor is there any surefire system. A system may work for a while and then suddenly stop working.

Being successful in the options market depends on you! Too

many investors seek out a guru who will make all their decisions; they will not take responsibility for their own actions. The only way to "make it" in the option markets is to earn it. Use the wisdom of the experts, but make your own decisions and be willing to take the responsibility for those decisions. No one will lead you to the promised land except you!

Secret

10

SECRET
PREDICTION
METHODS

In Secret #6. we discussed the almost impossible task of predicting futures and stock prices. However, out there are some methods that will improve your ability to predict the future; in other words, crystal balls that work sometimes. We live in a problematic world where there are no sure things, but there are ways to bend the odds in your favor where you are right about the future more often than you are wrong.

We are in the midst of a technological revolution. In the next two decades computers will probably become more intelligent than humans. This is due to the fact that microprocessors' speed doubles every eighteen months and has for the past thirty years. The explosion in technological development will accelerate as the computer becomes more intelligent.

Forecasting techniques that have developed due to this revolution include neural nets and genetic algorithms. These techniques are only possible with high-powered computers, which are now even in the home.

Neural nets use a methodology similar to how our brains work and identify patterns in data that cannot be identified by the naked eye.

Genetic algorithms is an evolutionary process similar to how we evolved from microorganisms over millions of years. With super fast and powerful computers, the evolutionary process can be replicated on the computer.

One company, Ward Systems, has trading systems software that use neural nets and have developed a specific software that may give you an edge. We also have experimented with neural nets in predicting stock index moves and have formed systems that predict market moves about 60% of the time. Nevertheless, because even neural nets can only have a small porthole on the future, this *still* tells us that the markets approach randomness.

Besides, these artificial intelligence tools, such as neural nets, do require a lot of work and a lot of continued retraining to implement.

Furthermore, even with these futuristic techniques for predicting the markets, when too many people use these methods and millions of dollars are poured into this process, the markets will become even more efficient and the future less predictable.

You may be able to develop a system that finds a peep hole on the future, but that could take a lot of work and continued retuning of your system.

Here, again, the advantage of options trading comes through; you don't have to predict the future.

11
MAVERICK INVESTING

To truly predict what the markets will do in the future, you need to look at the field of psychology and group behavior.

Since the start of the NYSE, it is well known that specialists who make a market in listed stocks make a lot of money each year. Why? Because they are forced to buy stock when prices are falling and sell stocks when prices are rising. Their job is to make a market in a stock, which means they must buy stock when everyone wants to sell and sell stock when everyone wants to buy. This forces them to be on the other side of the crowd. Emotionally they prefer not to be in that position. In fact, when the market is falling, they would prefer to be also sellers. The specialists in a sense have been forced to be contrary investors in the very short term. Consequently, in the end they are the winners.

Markets at times tend to move to extremes. When they do, you have a chance to stack the odds in your favor and improve your odds of predicting future price moves. The problem is that when markets move to extremes, you, like everyone else, emotionally don't want to take an opposing position. Despite this aversion, ironically, the best time to buy stocks is when there is blood in the streets and when in the pit of your stomach, you feel the world is about to end.

Markets tend to overshoot and undershoot their true value and at times become irrational as we saw in the internet crash in 2000. Here it is easy to predict the future, if you have the guts to go against the psychology of the crowd.

However, to be a successful contrary investor or maverick investor, you must be patient and wait for the real extremes. Buy when there is a lot of fear in the market and sell when there is a lot of euphoria and greed in the market. You also must control your greed in the midst of a bull market and control your fear at the bottom of the market.

One indication of whether the stock market is near a bottom is the CBOE Market Volatility Index (VIX). This index measures the implied volatility of the S&P 100 Index Options and, as a result, is a good measure of the fear in the market.

When implied volatility is high, options are expensive. This is because when there is a lot of fear in the market, investors buy put options, forcing put prices up, making options more expensive, and the VIX measures how expensive options are. The higher the VIX, the more fear there is in the market.

The index moving above 35% suggests that we are near a market bottom. (There is one exception to this rule. If the market is really volatile, the VIX should be high to reflect that volatility. Then the VIX will not be as predictive.)

Knowing how fear and euphoria work in the market and using it *for you* rather than *against you* is a self-discipline you have to acquire. Emotionally as well as intellectually, you have to prepare yourself for the game.

TRACKS IN THE CHARTS

12
TRACKS IN
THE CHARTS

Even though the markets approach randomness, technical charts of stocks or futures can provide some clues or tracks to what will happen in the future. However, readings from the charts are never a sure thing and should always be taken with a grain of salt.

Many traders take factual data too seriously, and many get lost in the trees. A chart of a stock's price action including its trading volume should be treated as signs in the sand of what the future might hold. Charts are pictures of supply and demand. They show you the trend and where the price will find support and resistance.

I look closely at support and resistance when designing my strategies, especially when setting stop-losses and profit goals. I also watch for breakouts from tight trading ranges. This supports a major change in volatility and improved odds of a major move.

Nevertheless, this again is not a sure thing. I put much more importance on trends when there is a lot of volume and no news to support the move.

Charts are not crystal balls but can provide signs to what may happen in the future, especially when they are not supported by news items and they are seen as a picture of supply and demand. They tell you where the money is flowing. For example, a stock price falling below long term support, or a place where it has found a lot of support in the past, suggests that a lot of money is flowing out of the stock and the stock price is likely to continue falling.

When a stock or futures makes a new high, it is likely to move higher for the resistance is rare at the level of a new high. There is no one left who is desperate to sell at a new high; i.e. no one still *hanging on* who was left *holding the bag* on the last major run up in the stock or futures.

However, there are buyers in line waiting *to jump on the band wagon* on any pull back. Likewise, when a stock or futures is making a new low, it is likely to move lower, for on any rally, sellers who were left *holding the bag* are waiting in line to get out.

Action in the charts becomes more valuable when there is no news to support the price action. Because the charts can tell you something is happening behind the scenes that the public is not aware of, they become crystal balls. This is where the slogan, "Buy on the rumor and sell on the news, " comes into play.

How good are charts at predicting the future? Well, they sure beat fundamentals. The charts were giving "sell" signals on stocks such as Enron, WorldCom and Adelphia Communications long before their demise. Fundamentals told you to sell when these stocks were almost worthless. In fact, when large brokerage firms give sell signals on stocks, most of the damage to the stock price has already been done. The answers are in the charts, not in the fundamentals.

Option prices can also foretell the future. When option premiums on a stock are suddenly very expensive and overpriced even though the stock price is not moving much, you should be suspicious. It suggests a news event or development that has not been exposed to the public.

In conclusion, the charts can foretell the future if you are a good detective and don't get lost in every tick of the tape. Despite this, remember, there are no sure things in the charts, just hints about what the future holds.

MAVERICK INVESTOR

13
USE THE
LAWS OF
SUPPLY AND
DEMAND

When dealing with commodities and commodity options, the laws of economics can be a valuable predictive tool. Here, again, you use extremes to predict the future.

Unlike stock—where a large number of variables determine the performance of a stock price—commodities' prices usually will comply closely with the laws of supply and demand.

For example, many years ago there was a freeze in the Southeast that killed off almost 1/3 of all the orange trees in several states. This resulted in orange juice prices racing up from $1.25 per pound to over $2.20 per pound, and a 1-cent move is equal to $150 on one contract; therefore a sizable move. However, a large amount of orange juice is produced in Brazil. Hence, with such a high price for orange juice, large quantities of Brazilian imports drove the price down to $1.00 per pound—far below where it started its rally.

Here we see the laws of supply and demand in action. When prices get too high, purchasers stop buying or find substitutes, and suppliers rush in to take advantage of these high prices. As a result, demand dries up and supply greatly increases, causing the commodity to fall in price, sometimes dramatically, as in the case of orange juice.

The reverse is true when prices are really low. Demand increases, due to a low price, but supply dries up because farmers or suppliers don't want to sell their goods at low prices. Therefore, farmers will stop growing the crop that is low in price, and eventually the price must rise.

However, sometimes other factors will delay this process. For example, several years in the 1980's, copper was selling for about 50-cents an ounce, far below production costs. Why? Third World nations that had copper reserves were desperately producing copper below cost in order to make the interest payments on their huge Third World loans from Western nations. This long hiatus caused many U.S. copper mines to shut down. Eventually, the low copper price and the removal of copper mines from production caused copper to run up above $1.50 an ounce, but it took a long while for the laws of supply and demand to kick in.

The laws of supply and demand are laws of science. Eventually, they will work in the market place, so, as an option player, try to use these to your advantage. You may say, "Why don't I just buy the futures contract, put down a small good faith deposit and wait, instead of paying an option premium?" Well, the big problem is how high is high and how low is low? If you think a commodity price is really low and you buy a futures contract, you have extensive risk if it keeps falling in price.

For example, at one time sugar dropped down to 5-cents a pound, and everyone said it could not go any lower. Well, it dropped down to 2-cents a pound, and each cent is equal to $1120. So, when you purchase a futures contract to catch the low, it is like trying to catch a falling knife; you can get hurt.

Options, because of their limited risk, are ideal for taking a position if a commodity is really high or really low in price. If you buy a call and the futures price still falls, all you can lose is the money you paid for the option; then, once it expires, you can roll into a new position, and if you use patience, you will eventually hit that home run.

If you plan to buy commodity options when commodities are too high or too low in price, you must be really patient, waiting for the ideal time to buy, then waiting for the option to pay off and, if it expires, rolling into a new option position—waiting for that home run when the laws of supply and demand kick in.

14

SELL IN MAY AND GO AWAY

"Sell in May and go away," is an adage on Wall Street that refers to the fact that stock prices tend to fall in May through September. A review of the past fifty years shows that holding stocks only from October till the start of May showed 10 times greater gains than holding stocks only from May till September.

Seasonal tendencies in stock and futures prices are an important predictive tool. For example, based on past studies, the market tends to decline in May and June and also September and October.

In fact, almost all stock market crashes occurred in October, including the crash of 1929, the crash of 1987, the crash of 1989, and the crash of 1997. No question that the best time to buy stocks is near the end of October.

One reason is that tax-loss selling by institutions occurs in

October. Also, stock prices tend to fall in December due to tax-loss selling by individual investors.

Another important seasonal tendency that has existed since the 1920's is *the end of the month phenomenon*. Stock prices tend to rise on the last trading day of the month and the first four days of the month.

In fact, if you had invested in the stock market averages only during those five days since the 1920's, you would have shown better gains than if you had been in the market the whole time. On those five magical days, stock prices rise 70% of the time during bull markets and 50% of the time during bear markets.

Why? One reason is that pension and market fund managers receive distributions from employee paychecks at the end of the month and must invest those funds.

Another seasonal tendency is that stock prices tend to rise on the day before a holiday. Why? First, professionals do not like to hold short positions over a holiday, especially if it includes a weekend, and will buy back their position before the holiday. In addition, many professionals start the holiday early, leaving only small investors who tend to buy instead of sell stock.

Seasonal tendencies also apply to futures and commodities. For example, based on a past study that spanned ten to fourteen years, corn prices (based on weekly nearby futures) tend to make their highs for the year in June or July and make their lows in December; soybeans make their highs in May and lows in October and November; wheat prices tend to make their highs in December and January and lows in May; cattle tends to make its highs in April and May and lows in July; hogs tends to make its highs from June through August and lows in November and December.

As you can see, seasonal tendencies should be considered when dealing with either commodities and futures or stocks. You have to take advantage and consider every tool at your disposal to play this game well.

15

THE 60% RULE

Even with all the predictive tools we have presented, the markets still approach randomness, at least for the regular investor. Unfortunately, a high percentage of investors believe they can predict the markets even though they can't. Yes, Lady Luck will make many investors think they have a crystal ball at least for a while, but in the end most will *pay the piper*.

Over the next two decades, as computers become more intelligent and even surpass human intelligence, most news and future events will be discounted in the markets long before they will occur. Hence, the only factors that will move the market and stock prices will be surprising unpredictable events.

Thus, the investor is better off to assume that the markets move randomly than to believe that he can predict the unpredictable. In fact, the stronger you think that an event is likely to occur, the more likely that you will be wrong.

When everyone believes in my prediction of the future, I know I'm in trouble.

Based on this premise and knowing that the predictive tools that I have presented only give me an edge, not a certainty, I always apply my 60% rule to my predictions of what a stock or commodity or the market will do. That rule assumes that I will only be right 60% of the time no matter how I feel about a position or projection. The rule forces me to design option strategies that will pay off even if I am only right 60% or less of the time.

Most investors think they can outguess what stocks and the market will do. However, since 90% of the money managers can't beat the market and the indexes, investors would be wiser to assume the markets are random and invest accordingly.

The best way to invest in stocks is to buy a low-fee index fund or an exchange- traded index such as the Nasdaq 100 (QQQ) or the S&P 500 (SPY), and do this by dollar averaging; in other words, putting the same number of dollars in the market each month (probably in the third week of the month). Then you are participating in the long term growth of stocks without having to predict what will happen next week or next month, for once you try to time the markets, you are doomed.

Remember, in the long run, you will probably only be right at the most 60% of the time, so adjust your strategies accordingly. The beauty of options is that if you design the right strategies, you can be wrong about the markets often and still profit.

Secret

16

PREDICTING STOCK TOPS AND MARKET BOTTOMS

The technical charts can also provide clues for when a stock is near or about to make a top. The secret, here, is the stock's volume. When a stock price has been in a strong uptrend and then suddenly shows extremely high volume—yet the stock's price shows no upward progress—there is a good probability the stock is making a top or is near a top. If you own the stock or calls on the stock, it is time to take profits.

My rule of thumb is that the volume must be extremely high for two or three days in a row. Corinthian Colleges (COCO) is a stock where I recommended a put option in the summer of 2001, based on this phenomenon. Over the next month, COCO dropped from 51 to 25.

The secret to determining when the market hits bottom or a temporary bottom is to measure the amount of panic in the market. One classic line is "only buy when there is blood in the streets" or when in the pit of the stomach, you feel the world is coming to an end. This is, indeed, the time to buy.

One easy way to measure such panic is to look at two indexes, the CBOE Volatility Index (VIX) and the Nasdaq Volatility Index (VNX). The CBOE Volatility Index measures the implied volatility of the puts and calls of the S&P 100 Index (OEX). The Nasdaq Volatility Index measures the implied volatility of puts and calls of the Nasdaq 100 Index. The higher the implied volatility, the more expensive the options.

During market declines, investors buy more put options, driving up the price of options and, therefore, their implied volatility. The implied volatility getting extremely high is a sign of panic in the market. Sometimes it takes a few weeks to reach that bottom, but when the VIX and VNX are extremely high, it is time to start entering bullish strategies.

One warning, however, the VIX and VNX must be at extremes. For example, after the tragic World Trade Center events of September 11, 2001, the VIX hit a high of over 57%

One final comment here. Bottoms are made when the sellers are exhausted. This occurs when a stock stops dropping in price on very high volume. For example, when WorldCom collapsed, the stock price dropped to 7-cents and stopped moving down on huge volume. Knowing that even bankrupt stocks will hold a small premium, and that 7-cents was the bottom of that market where the sellers would be exhausted, I bought the stock at 7-cents and sold it the next day for 24-cents a share.

Section 3
Option Buying

Secret

17

GET THE BIGGEST BANG FOR YOUR BUCK

Buying options is the best way to start trading options. The big advantage that you have is that you can't lose more than you pay for the option. That is not true of some other option strategies such as option writing.

The major error made by option buyers and the reason some take big losses is that they pay too much for their options. In fact, most option authorities recommend buying in-the-money options where the stock price is across the strike price. The problem with these options is that they have high price tags, usually several hundred dollars to a thousand dollars and sometimes more. There is a place for this type of action, but when you are aiming for high profits, you need a different strategy.

In addition, when you pay a high price for an option, you have a lot at risk; one wrong move of the underlying stock or futures and most of your option premium could vanish. If you pay very little for an option, if the stock moves the wrong way, you won't lose much. Also, the higher the price, the smaller the chance of a big percentage gain.

Cheaper options, in addition, give you a much bigger bang for your buck. With cheap options, percentage gains of over 1000% are not unusual. You can buy options for as little as $5.00 (.05), the cost of a cup of coffee in the morning, and the $5.00 controls 100 shares of stock.

I set a guideline to avoid paying more than 2 ($200) for any stock option and $400 for any futures option. Then I know that I have a chance for a big percentage gain or a home run and I am getting the biggest bang for my buck.

18

BEWARE OF INERTIA

Another problem with expensive options is that almost all investors suffer from inertia. When you own expensive options, you should have a stop-loss price on the underlying stock or futures price. If that stop-loss price is hit, you should sell your option immediately.

However, most investors do not use stops and do not like to take losses. Consequently, when the stock makes the wrong move or doesn't move at all, the option trader watches his expensive option fade away.

As one of my students once said, options (unlike stocks) are like melting ice cubes. They depreciate as time passes. With stock you are given a second chance; you can wait for the stock price to return to profitability. Inertia works in your favor. However, with options you are not given a second chance. For option buyers, time is your enemy. If the stock price moves against you, you must act or you will see the price you paid for that option melt away. Ninety percent of all investors will not act, and you are probably in that category.

The big advantage of cheap options is that you have an automatic stop-loss. If the stock or futures price does not move according to your predictions, the options will expire and you will lose the small amount you paid for the option. Then inertia will not hurt you very much.

19

CHEAP IS NOT ALWAYS CHEAP!

Cheap options are easily found. Just look in your financial newspaper or on the internet, and there are hundreds and thousands of options that are priced under 1 ($100). However, to be successful, you must buy options that are not only cheap, but also bargains or underpriced options. The vast majority of cheap options are overpriced or really worthless. The way to success is to find cheap options that are also undervalued or bargains that should be going for higher prices.

We will spend a lot of time in this book showing you how to identify bargain options. When you can find such bargains, your ability to predict what the underlying stock or futures will do is not as important because the risk-reward picture will be so attractive that even if you are right only 30% of the time, you will be a winner. If you remember, my track record in the 1980's showed a 1500% return during two years, but only 20% of the options paid off during those years.

Consequently, your objective should be to identify options that are both cheap and underpriced or bargained priced.

**WHEN BUYING OPTIONS SWING FOR THE FENCES
WITH CHEAP, UNDERVALUED OPTIONS.**

20
SWING FOR
THE FENCES

There is an old adage on Wall Street that says, "Never be afraid to take a profit," but with options this adage does not apply. As an option buyer, your major goal should be to hit a home run. You can't afford to nickel and dime your way to profits. Too many of your options will expire or lose most of their value, and your nickel and dime profits will not be able to offset those losses.

Home runs are best defined as options that return 500% to 1000% returns. When you buy cheaper options, you have the ability to hit home runs.

For example, in my newsletter, *The Complete Option Report*, in August of 1987, I recommended a December ITT 55 put at 1/8 when ITT was 65. A price of 1/8 is $12.50 per 100 shares, so you could control 100 shares of ITT for the cost of breakfast. Why did I select this item? Because it had a theoretical value of .5 or

$50.00. In other words, it was undervalued, a true bargain. I liked the position so much I included it in an option article for the newsletter.

Of course, in October we saw the crash of '87, and ITT dropped to 47. The ITT dropped 8 points beyond the strike price of the ITT 55 put, giving it an intrinsic value of 8 ($800). However, the panic in the market pushed the price of this option to 16 ($1600). As a result, for a $12.50 investment plus commission, you could have made $1600, over a 10,000% return. That means your next 100 option positions could expire worthless and you still would have a profit.

Here is the magic of the home run; just one or two home runs can pay for a lot of strikeouts and mistakes made by the option trader. However, hitting the home runs requires tremendous patience and good trading tactics.

Secret

21

LET IT RIDE!

Your goal, as established in Secret #20, is to hit home runs in order to offset and, in fact, get above the many losses you will inevitably have, especially if you buy cheap, out-of-the-money options. You have to hit home runs in order to insure that your bottom line will have a profit. To hit the home runs, you must let part of your position ride, aiming for greater gains.

However, that is not to say that when your options show a profit, you shouldn't take some money off the table. My rule here is to take profits on half of any position when your option doubles in price, and let the rest ride!

A GOOD OPTION TRADER IS A GUNSLINGER-WITH A TRIGGER FINGER-QUICK TO TAKE PROFITS AND CUT LOSSES.

22

DON'T LET PROFITS SLIP AWAY

A major sin of an option player is to let a big profit slip away. You must swing for the fences and go for the home runs, but you must also protect the paper profits already in your position, which is a difficult task. Therefore, stop-losses are critical, and scaling out of a position as it moves in your direction is a wise tactic. Here, you also need a trigger finger ready to capture the rest of your profits when you see signs of a reversal.

Once you have a good paper profit, always set a trailing stop-loss on the underlying security or futures. A 5% stop-loss is a good rule of thumb. In other words, if the underlying stock price is 50, set a stop-loss of 47.5. If the stock price hits 47.5, take profits on the rest of your position.

Also, sometimes a tighter stop-loss may be appropriate. Ratchet up your stops as the underlying stock moves in your direction, keeping them away from the present stock or index price. However, even if the stop-loss is not hit, you may still exit a position if you think the underlying stock or futures is flattening out and when you believe it has hit some resistance or support. (Check the charts.)

I can't emphasize enough how important quick action is necessary when things start turning against you. With options, due to their short life, you are usually only given one chance to get out. *If you hesitate, you are lost !*

23

BEAT THE CLOCK

When you are an option buyer, the passage of time is your greatest enemy. When you own options, time flies. It always seems that the stock or futures makes the move you need the day after the option expires.

In our research, time seems to be the most valuable asset of an option. Given enough time, most stock or futures will make a major move, giving you a home run. If you can find a cheap and undervalued option with a lot of time, you have a great investment. Cheap, long term options, where the strike price is in range of the underlying stock or futures price, are true gems in the rough.

The point to remember here is to buy enough time, for time flies. Options depreciate as time passes, so, the refrain, buy enough time!

Also, always set a time limit on how long you will hold an

option. If nothing happens within that time period, exit the position. With more expensive options and in-the-money options, I usually set a three week hold period. After three weeks, I am out of that position.

24

AVOID AN OPTION'S LAST MONTH

As a general rule, I avoid holding options in their last month before expiration. They depreciate at the fastest rate during that last month. In fact, in some cases the option premiums absolutely collapse.

One reason such depreciation may occur is because option investors sell (write) options the last month before expiration. In fact, I write options a day or two before the last month begins (expiration of the previous month). Nevertheless, sometimes I buy options with one month or less before expiration if they are extremely cheap and undervalued and if the underlying stock or futures price is close to the strike price.

This strategy gives you a secret advantage that we will cover in a future chapter; no further explanation of this secret is needed now. Unless there is a little premium to salvage, just get out of option positions before the last month.

25

THE SECRET OF SCALING

Try to scale into positions and out of positions. As you enter an option position, take a few small steps; initially take a small position and then add to it as the underlying moves in price, always making sure you are getting good value for your options.

However, never take a huge position. Make sure any option position is less than 5% of your total option buying portfolio. Also, if you find a super bargain, forget about scaling and take what you can get!

Scaling out of a position is the secret to never losing a good paper profit. Gradually take profits as the option position moves in your direction. Sell a few options when they double in price, sell some more when they triple in price and so on, leaving just a few options for a potential super spectacular move.

Scaling out is one way to insure that you will not lose the profits already in your position. Scaling, of course, requires that you buy more than one option to a position. Try to buy at least three options to each position you take.

Secret

26

BEWARE OF DELUSIONS OF GRANDEUR

Most option buyers have totally unrealistic expectations. There is a tremendous amount of hype about how much you can make buying options. Many option experts promise 100% and even 1000% returns each year. Unfortunately, most option investors lose, and most get discouraged very quickly when their dream of quick riches vanishes.

Option buying is a very tough game that requires tremendous patience. Your goal should be to make a profit, period, each year, and that may be tougher than you think. Forget about fabulous returns.

I have been writing an option advisory newsletter ever since 1983, and in some of these years, we showed extremely high returns. However, those returns are theoretical returns, and theoretical returns are hard to convert to real returns. Only the most skilled player can do so and do so by rigidly following many of the rules that we have discovered.

The problem with unrealistic expectations is that in your attempt at extremely high returns, you make the wrong plays and take far more risks than you should. You're not patient and make the wrong moves. Also, you are unable to handle long losing streaks that you are sure eventually to face. The most likely result is that you will give up after a few losses.

Option buying requires a lot of staying power and your ability to handle a lot of losses and still stay in the game. Unrealistic expectations will not do that!

27

DON'T PLUNGE!

After trading stocks and options for over thirty years, I have found that the one glaring error made by both successful and unsuccessful traders is that at one point in their life they plunged into the market, betting everything on one position that they considered a sure thing.

Of course, that sure thing didn't pan out, and they lost almost everything. In fact, the more sure you are about an event occurring, the less likely it will happen—the basis of the contrary theory.

For example, I had a good friend, a former financial advisor, who was sure the market was going to crash in 1987, so he took his whole portfolio and purchased put options with everything he had. Well, the market did crash, and if it had crashed one week earlier, he would have made millions. Unfortunately, all of his options expired worthless, and he lost everything. Here, following our secret of scaling, he could have saved some of the bacon.

Two years later, another friend, a financial planner, did the same. He put all his cash into put options, betting the market would crash, but the market reversed, and he watched all of his options vanish.

Many of the top traders in the world have faced the same crisis when they played in the market, chasing the "sure thing". (I suggest you read *Market Wizards* by Jack D. Schwager.)

These traders paid a high price for a valuable lesson. You don't have to pay this tuition if you don't plunge. Spread out your purchases over time and position, and never bet everything on that sure thing.

THE NOTICE INVESTOR BLINDLY TAKES THE "ANY HORSE IN A BARN WILL DO" APPROACH TO SELECTING OPTION STRATEGIES.

28 ANALYZE YOUR OPTION POSITION

Beware of the "any horse in a barn" approach to option buying. Ninety percent of all option buyers approach the option markets totally wrong. They think a stock or futures will move up or down and randomly select any option they can find on that stock or futures without carefully analyzing the option position and determining whether it is a good or bad play.

A classic error made by option buyers is to see the underlying stock, index or futures move the way they have predicted but to purchase an underlying option that does not increase in value at all. One option buyer bought a call with a strike price of 20 for a price of 1 when the stock was 13. The stock did rise to 20 at expiration, but the option never rose above the price paid for it and expired worthless. Options have their own risk-reward picture, and you must understand that picture before entering a position.

The beauty with options is that you can mathematically measure what an option is worth and what your probability of profit will be. In fact, the mathematical model for measuring the real worth of an option won a Nobel Prize in Economics in 1997.

We will discuss option analysis in future chapters, but the process of option analysis is easier than you think. To do it properly, a computer is required, but even a Palm hand-held computer would do for about a $100 investment.

These three items are what you need to know as you compare options in order to select the best one to buy:

1. The fair price of an option
2. The probability of profit
3. The delta

How do you use this information? Try to buy options where the option is under the fair price. Know that the higher the probability of profit and the higher the delta, the better the play.

But, what is the delta? The delta tells you how the option will move if the stock or futures increases 1 point. For example, if the delta is .30 and if the stock increases 1 point, the option will increase 30% of a point or .30.

There are many computer programs that will provide this output, including *Option Master*®, which also works on a Palm system.

If these three items do not look good, look for another option or create a strategy that has a good risk-reward picture, (to be covered in a future chapter). If I can't find a good play on the underlying stock or futures, I pass the position or just play the underlying stock or futures without using options.

29

THE SECRET OF PROFIT BOXES

Many option buyers purchase options that are at or in-the-money. These options have much higher deltas and move much closer with the underlying stock or futures.

There are serious disadvantages with these options. Not only are they quite expensive, where several hundred or thousands of dollars are at stake, but one wrong move by the underlying stock or futures and the option price will collapse, losing you thousands of dollars.

Furthermore, unlike stock, you do not usually have a second chance or the time for the stock price to come back. As a result, you need to create a game plan that provides you with some protection.

In my newsletter, *The Put and Call Tactician*, we create Option Profit Boxes. The Profit Box is a game plan where if the underlying stock or futures price stays in the Profit Box, you stay in the option position, but if the underlying stock or futures leaves the Box, you immediately exit the position.

The beauty with the Profit Box is that you are only in the position for a maximum of three weeks and you have a very tight stop-loss. You exit if the underlying stock or futures starts to move in the wrong direction.

Check out the examples in Secret #66.

With such a strategy, you are in the position for a short time to avoid the danger of time decay of the option and a lot of loss in the option value. This strategy gives you the chance to exit if the underlying stock or futures moves in the wrong direction.

This game plan also counters the tendency of the option buyer to suffer from inertia. As an option buyer, as you already know, one of your greatest enemies is inertia. You need to be quick on the trigger when you take profits or cut losses. The Profit Boxes help you with the process.

Secret

30

THE STRADDLE SECRET

A straddle is a form of option buying where you buy both a put and a call on the same underlying stock or futures, both with the same strike price and expiration month. Then the underlying can move either up or down to win, and sometimes you can win on both sides.

I am not usually a great fan of straddles because their price tag is usually pretty high and you could be stuck with an expensive option position. If the underlying stock or futures does not move, you could take a beating.

However, if you can find a cheap straddle with plenty of time, you could find a strategy with a high probability of generating a profit, and that is very rare for a position where you have limited risk. In other words, you cannot lose more than you paid for the positions (the put and call).

For example, in 2001, one of my plays of the week in *Ultimate Option Strategies* was a straddle on the stock, Terra Networks, where you bought the Dec 7.5 call and 7.5 put. The combined price of the two options was 1.5. This means that Terra Networks would have to drop to 6 to break even (7.5 − 1.5 = 6) or rise to 9 to break even (7.5 + 1.5 = 9).

To analyze this position, we ran a computer simulation to determine the probability of one of our profit points being hit during the life of the trade. This analysis is only possible through computer simulation, and such simulation can be done on *Option Master® Deluxe* software. Based on that analysis, we found that there was a 80% probability of showing a profit some time during the life of the options.

In addition, I looked at the charts and made sure Terra Networks, an internet stock, had been an extremely volatile stock in the past. In September of 2001, the stock dropped down to 5, generating a good profit for the position.

Two internet programs that will help you find good straddles are *The Power Analyzer* and *The Option Research Scanner*, available at *options-inc.com*. Nevertheless, once you find what looks like a good straddle, make sure you run a simulation on the straddle and only enter such trades where you have an 80% or better probability of profit. Most of the straddles I have recommended over the years have been profitable, probably due to the fact we only selected straddles with over an 80% probability of profit.

(We will cover simulations in a later chapter, and in the Option Analysis section of the book.)

Finding a good straddle is only half the game. Taking profits on such trades is your next challenge. Here apply the rules we discussed previously. When you have a profit, scale out of positions and set tight trailing stop-losses so profits won't slip away. Also, when you take profits on one side of the position, you may wish to sell the other side if there is some option premium left.

31

BE PATIENT

"Patience and perseverance have a magical effect before which difficulties disappear and obstacles vanish."
—John Quincy Adams

One of the most important attributes of a professional option trader is patience, the patience to wait for the good trade and the patience to handle a lot of losses and wait for the big profits. I cannot over emphasize the importance of being patient. Most option investors will jump impetuously into option trades, looking for action rather than looking for sound trades.

You need the patience to find an option play with a good risk-reward picture, and then you need the patience to wait for the profits! Few option buyers have this attribute.

THE OPTION BUYER'S SECRET WEAPON
-THE SHOCK AND AWE OF STOCK PRICE
ACTION-SURPRISE VOLATILITY!

32

THE OPTION BUYER'S SECRET WEAPON— SHOCK AND AWE

This is one of the most important secrets in the book. Many option experts have said that option buying is the sucker's game and most professionals are option writers. This is partially true. I love to write options, but option buyers have one secret advantage. That advantage is *surprise volatility*. You see, when you buy options, you are betting on one thing—volatility, movement of the underlying stock or futures price. If the stock does not move, you lose!

Volatility is usually pretty predictable and moves in accordance with a log normal curve (i.e. bell curve). In fact, the Black and Scholes Pricing Model for measuring the fair value of an option, which won a Nobel Prize, is based on this curve.

The problem is that the markets do not always move in accordance with a log normal curve. Chaos theory throws a wrench in the bell curve theory. Stocks and even futures can make moves that are much larger than what a log normal curve prescribes.

For example, over the past few years, many stocks have made 5 to 10 point moves, sometimes more overnight, and on some occasions dropping over 50% in value, based on unexpected news, earnings reports or takeover action.

On a log normal curve, there are 3 standard deviations on each side of the curve, but some stocks move as much as 10 standard deviations, way beyond the bounds of the curve. Hence, the pricing model is undervaluing the options, especially the out-of-the-money ones at the ends of the curve. In statistical terms, the tails of the curve are fat.

Therefore, *surprise* events prescribed in chaos theory can create instant home runs for option buyers and provide the option buyer with a secret edge in the game.

One reason for the gigantic moves in stock prices, usually overnight, is the institutional influence. There are over 4000 mutual funds, and the institutions truly dominate the stock market.

Hence, when a negative news item comes out about a stock, the institutions—like a herd of elephants trying to exit through a small door—try to exit the stock at the same time and cause the stock to show a dramatic drop in price; for institutional managers do not want to show a losing stock in their portfolio.

In conclusion, when you are buying options, buy options on stocks that have the greatest potential for *surprise* volatility. That would mean tech stocks, overvalued stocks with a lot of hype, single drug pharmacy stocks up for FDA review, stocks in industries that are in flux, stocks where you cannot pronounce the name, and the list goes on, any stock or futures that is vulnerable to surprise news or events.

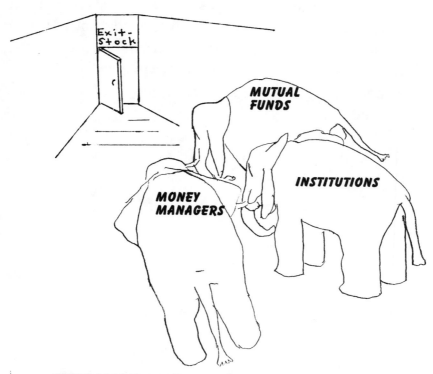

WHEN BAD NEWS HITS, INSTITUTIONS RUSH TO EXIT A
STOCK LIKE A HERD OF ELEPHANTS TRYING TO EXIT
THROUGH A SMALL DOOR.

33

THE STOCK ADVANTAGE

As you search for the best options to buy, you have a choice of stocks, indexes or futures, both financial and commodities. Which one has the greatest potential for surprise volatility? The winner is stocks!

Stocks by far have the potential for surprise price action. If you review and compare the historical volatility of stocks, indexes and futures, you will see the difference. In fact, some stocks have natural volatility of over 100%. Never will you see that with other instruments. Stocks are much more prone to explosive gains and losses.

Therefore, there is a big advantage to buying options on stocks rather than other instruments, such as futures. Also, again remember, when you buy options, you are betting on volatility, so buy options on those instruments that have the greatest potential for surprise movements.

Secret

34
THE PUT ADVANTAGE

When you buy options, you should always buy both puts and calls. However, based on our research and track record over seventeen years—even though we recommended the same number of puts and calls for stocks—the put investments by far provided the best return with the most home runs.

Therefore, I would bias my options portfolio with more puts than calls. Puts provide more home runs for stocks, not only due to surprise volatility, but also to the fact that when stocks fall, panic can set in and enhance the decline. And, of course, there is the institutional influence.

Many years ago Joe Granville and I were discussing our love for put options, and he made a good analogy. When stocks rise in price, it is like climbing the steps of the Empire State Building, but when they fall, it is like jumping off the Empire State Building. Stock prices fall much more sharply than they rise, and that is what you are betting on—violent price action. Consequently, puts give you more bang for your buck.

There is also another advantage; puts are usually cheaper than calls. This is due to the fact that puts and calls are priced based on the cost of holding the underlying position and a call is a surrogate for the stock. Owning a stock is more expensive than shorting a stock, the purpose of a put.

35 DIVERSIFY

Diversification, important in all investments, is critical when it comes to option buying. Since many of your positions will be losers, the more positions you have increases your odds of hitting a home run. With only a few positions, you could easily wipe out your portfolio very quickly.

When we talk about diversification, we generally mean you should own both puts and calls and a variety of each, but there is another type of diversification that also applies here—DIVERSIFY OVER TIME!

Don't buy a lot of option positions at one time. You are betting on market volatility. If the market goes to sleep (and it can sometimes for a year or so), you are dead. Your options will melt away and expire. If all your money is in options at one time, your portfolio will vanish.

Therefore, you want to enter option positions gradually over time, patiently waiting for the market or a stock to explode. Once you see the market waking up, you can increase your option buying activity.

A good game tactic is to plan to spend a set amount of dollars each year and gradually to invest that capital over that period, possibly using seasonal tendencies to maximize your opportunities and gains.

Time diversity is also important, for you are sure to encounter losing streaks, and when you do, you will have enough money in reserve to return and play another day.

THE QUICK AND THE DEAD

36

THE QUICK
AND THE
DEAD

Option buying is a great game. It has that secret edge of surprise volatility in stocks and gives you the opportunity of big payoffs. Nevertheless, option buying does require close surveillance and very quick actions on your part. One hesitation and you could lose all of your profit and all of your investment in a position.

Inertia is the greatest enemy of the option buyer. Afraid to take a loss or being too slow to capture a profit does in most option players. When you are trading options, time is your enemy. You are usually given only one chance to take a profit or cut a loss. If you are not quick enough, you are dead; there are no second chances.

37

THE SECRET OF PORTFOLIO INSURANCE

The easiest way to protect a stock portfolio from a market decline is to buy put options. If you already own a put portfolio as part of your option buying activities, you already have some built-in insurance.

Over the years in the many lectures and presentations that I have made, I have warned investors always to hold some puts in their portfolio in order to protect their stock positions and mutual funds from unexpected market declines. My reference has always been to the bear market of 1973–1974, where many large mutual funds lost 80% of their value.

Those warnings did not seem very believable to many investors until the bear market of 2000–2002 when many Nasdaq stocks dropped 90% in value and the disastrous attacks of September 11, 2001 sent the market into a nose dive.

Because of unpredictable variables, described in chaos theory, we never know what other event could send the market or individual stocks, such as the airlines, into a tailspin. Another terrorist attack, possibly on a greater magnitude, or a gigantic earthquake in a population center such as Southern California could see the market lose a quarter or more of its value. (An earthquake as recent as 1976 killed over 500,000 people in China.)

To add gasoline to the fire, there is evidence to support a potential depression. (Read Robert R. Prechter Jr. 's *Conquer the Crash.*) Such events are possible. Although we hope never to see such events in our future, we should be prepared for such uncertainties. Some theorists claim that a nuclear attack or gigantic earthquake in a major population center in the US is inevitable over the next twenty to fifty years.

Consequently, a put portfolio is not only a good speculation, but also a good insurance policy to offset some of the risk of your portfolio. We buy insurance for our home, our health, our automobile and even our vacations. Why not buy insurance for our portfolio that took a lifetime to develop?

Many saw much of their portfolio vanish in the severe bear market that started in 2000. What if they had had some put insurance?

However, most people have a tendency to buy too much insurance. You buy insurance for a potential disaster. You don't need total protection. What you need is a safety net. Buying cheap out-of-the-money puts can provide that net. Therefore, your put insurance will not be a big investment, just a very small percentage of your portfolio.

Nevertheless, when buying these puts, make sure they are undervalued and have a decent probability of profit and delta. Try to make your put portfolio a separate profit center even though it is designed as an insurance policy. Here is a rare occurrence where your insurance policy could actually generate a profit even if you don't see a disastrous decline. Puts purchased in such a portfolio do not have to be the same as the stocks you own. As a result, you can be a true bargain hunter.

You can also buy puts on the stocks you own, especially when a stock is vulnerable to a decline and you do not wish to sell the stock. Again, try to buy cheap out-of-the-money puts. They won't give full protection but will act like a deductible insurance policy, and for a small price you get a lot of reassurance.

Buying such puts may not be a good investment, but it will be when the market is in the depths of decline where you are ready to panic out of the market right at the wrong time. Puts will give you the reassurance that will enable you not only to sleep at night, but also to avoid panicking and selling your stock when you shouldn't, usually at a market bottom.

One observation I have made over the years is that sometimes you are given a second chance to buy some put insurance. During severe market declines if you act quickly, you sometimes can still buy puts at reasonable prices. Again, it is great to have puts in your portfolio just for peace of mind, but some sizable profits can be made, particularly during a severe market decline, if the situation is right.

For example, after the Twin Towers attack during the first day after the market opened, even though many stocks gapped down on the opening (i.e. the airlines), there were many stocks that temporarily held up in price that took much bigger hits in the next few days. There was time to buy puts that paid off big time. But, again, quick action is needed.

38

THE SECOND SECRET TO PORTFOLIO INSURANCE

Another way to buy stock and get insurance with it is to buy a structured product. There are financial instruments that trade like closed end funds where you are actually buying an index of stocks (i.e. S&P 500) (i.e. index mutual fund).

These instruments trade like a listed stock and can be bought and sold during the day. When you buy them, it is like buying a mutual fund (closed end), but they have a built-in insurance. They guarantee you a certain price when they mature, usually in five to six years, but you can trade them up to the day they mature.

Each of these instruments or structured products has different terms and a guarantee by one of the big brokerage houses. These structured products have strike prices like options and will rise at a similar rate to the underlying stock index. However, there is a cost for this insurance, usually reflected in a slightly smaller gain.

In the mid 90's, I bought shares of one of these instruments. It was the Stock Index Return Security (SIS), a structured product, that reflected the Mid Cap 400 Index. I paid $8.75 for each share and was guaranteed 10 at maturity. I sold my position several years later for about $32 a share.

Let's take a look at an example. Merrill Lynch has a structured product whose symbol is MLF that tracks the S&P 500 Index. Referred to as an S&P 500 "MITTS", the MLF are senior unsecured debt securities of Merrill Lynch. It has a strike price for the S&P 500 Index of 1011, but at expiration on 7-1-05 only gains in S&P 500 above 1119.49 would be reflected in the MLF price.

The difference reflects the cost of downside protection. The market price of the MLF was 9.94 on 4-24-02 when the S&P 500 Index was 1094, but the guaranteed price at expiration is 10 regardless of what the market does, even if the S&P 500 Index were to lose 50% or more of its value.

In other words, here is the way, in a sense, to buy a stock mutual fund without any downside risk due to a fall in the value of the index.

The MLF is traded on the American Stock Exchange along with most structured products. Before buying one of these securities, make sure to read the prospectus. For such information call 1-800-THE AMEX, or check their web site, *amex.com*.

As good as all this sounds, particularly when your concern is for insurance, you still have to be alert. Before purchasing shares in one of these structured instruments, do your homework. Always do your homework!

Secret

39
A LONG SHOT SECRET

For those players who like to play long shots, consider buying expiring options. During the last week before expiration, very-close-to-the-money options can make dramatic moves in value within one or two days. Buying such options can generate some real home runs.

The best options to buy here are index options, such as the S&P 100 Index (OEX) and the S&P 500 Index (SPX), for they give you the most bang for your buck in those last few days before expiration.

The key to success in this strategy is to buy on weakness in the option price. Try to buy options under 1 that are very close to the strike price.

Be warned, you will incur a lot of losses, but just one big move in the index price will give you a big jackpot. You may wish to play it on paper for a while to see the results of these types of play. Here, you are betting on *chaos theory's* surprise volatility.

Many years ago I was watching IBM move in a 3 point trading range each day as we approached expiration. The close-to-the-money call would move from 1 down to 1/8 with 2 days before expiration. Seeing this, I entered an order to purchase the call at 1/8 (.125). The order was filled during the day at 1/8. I, then, immediately put in an order to sell the option at 1. The order was filled a few hours later, giving us over a 700% gain, yet the option eventually expired worthless. The lesson is that fast action is needed with this strategy.

Now for the one that got away. Using this expiration strategy, I bought some call options on the S&P 100 Index one week before expiration at 3/8 (.38). Then with three days before expiration, I had to make an unexpected business trip, so I closed out the position at 3/4 (.75). At expiration the Index was 7 points ($700) in-the-money of the call option. If I would have held the position, my gain would have been almost 2000%.

If you use this strategy, make sure to buy the options really cheap—on weakness where there is still a fair chance the index or stock price could move across the strike price into-the-money.

You need a lot of patience and tolerance for losses to play this strategy, and there will be many months where you will not find opportunities. However, if the game is played correctly and you like long shots, this strategy can give you big rewards.

Section 4
Option Writing

THE OPTION WRITER TAKES THE BET INSTEAD OF MAKING THE BET

Secret

40

TAKE THE BET INSTEAD OF MAKING THE BET

The option markets provide that rare opportunity for the individual investor to be the bank, casino or legal bookie. In other words, you have the opportunity to take the bet rather than make the bet. Taking the bet refers to option writing—the direct opposite of option buying. The option writer is the one who takes and guarantees to pay off on the bet made by the option buyer.

When you go to the sports book in a casino in Nevada, the job title of the person who takes your bet on a football or basketball game is called a *sports writer*. The person who takes your bets when you play Keno in a casino is called a *Keno writer*.

Now you have the opportunity to be a *writer*, an *option writer*, where instead of buying an option, you sell an option and the option premium (price) goes directly into your account. Now, you have to pay off if the underlying stock or futures moves across the strike price and into-the-money.

The beauty with an option writer over a casino or bookie is that you have the ability to close the casino door. In other words, you have the ability to close out your position and obligation at any time by buying back the option.

For example, let's say that the IBM Dec 110 call is priced at 2 when the stock price is 100. You would write this option by entering an order to sell the Dec 110 call at 2 to open. When the order is executed, $200 goes into your account.

However, for the $200 you are obligated to deliver 100 shares of stock at $110 a share to an option buyer if he exercises your option. That would occur if IBM is at or above 110, especially at expiration. If IBM is below 110, the option will expire worthless; in either case you keep the $200. Of course, you can close the position out at any time before expiration by buying back the option.

Option writing can be played by all types of option investors from the conservative to the high risk-takers and in all cases can provide an excellent source of income. In fact, to be a professional option trader, you must do some option writing because it provides a consistent source of income.

41 THE SECRET ADVANTAGE OF OPTION WRITING

The secret advantage of option writing is that you can enter trades where you have a very high probability of winning no matter what the market, a stock or a futures does. In fact, you can sometimes enter a trade that has a 99% chance of winning. In a sense, at times, they are giving money away on the exchanges.

Why? The option writer usually wins if the underlying instrument moves in the direction you expect or stays still or moves against you very slowly. The only time the option writer gets hurt is when the underlying instrument makes a big quick move against you. The disadvantage to the option writer is the chance of a big loss, for you face unlimited risk.

42 THE SECRET TO QUICK PROFITS

The big advantage of option writing is that you win almost all the time and usually quickly. For the gladiator in the crowd who is out for fast profits, option writing is the only game in town. Writing short term options that have a high probability of profit can generate a lot of income for your portfolio quickly.

Unlike option buyers who have to wait and pray for a big return and rarely see a big winner, option writers sit back and collect the money and let the passing of time work for them. Option writing requires less surveillance and fewer decisions and actions than does option buying. All option writers have to do is write an option and watch it expire. Just once in a while they will get stopped out of their position.

The real aggressive option writers can pile up a lot of profit quickly, but they have to keep in mind that with such quick profits, there is always the chance of financial ruin. Regardless, option writing is the supreme game, and for the young, single, aggressive gladiators, it's a game they would want to play.

43

PLAY IT NAKED

The most aggressive option strategy is to write puts and calls naked without any type of hedge, such as owning the underlying stock or futures, or without buying some other options to hedge the risk. Such a strategy has unlimited or extreme risk and normally is for gladiators only.

Of course, you have the greatest potential reward, but even when you have a small position, the risk can be sizable. The greatest danger to writers occurs during a crash. For example, during the crash of 1987, one investor who was naked just 3 index puts saw a loss of $120,000 overnight.

Another investor started with $15,000 two years before that crash and made, writing naked index options, $750,000; this was still before the crash. However, on the day of the crash, he lost the $750,000 and 2 million more that he did not have.

These war stories demonstrate that you must always be on

the defensive. When at times I write naked puts and calls for speculation, I wait until I find an ideal situation. Having this ideal situation is necessary because, though naked writing can be a true advantage with a lot of reward, it is so dangerous that minimizing the risk as much as possible becomes very important. How to find the ideal situation will be forthcoming.

44

PROBABILITY— THE FIRST SECRET FOR OPTION WRITERS

From my experience the secret to winning at the naked option writing game is to find very high probability plays. I write naked options for speculation that have a very high probability of paying off. With software that is now available (i.e. *Option Master®*), you can measure the probability of a successful play.

Whenever you write naked options, you must use a stop-loss to survive. I use a stop-loss based on the underlying stock, index or futures, But even better, using a simulator, you can determine the probability of hitting the stop-loss during the life of the option.

I am always in search of a *sure thing*. Whenever the probability of success is greater than 90%, I have a potential play. The key to finding high probability plays is to write far-out-of-the-money options. My best play was a Cell Pathways (CLPA) 7.50 put priced at 1 ($100) with about 2 1/2 months before expiration, but the underlying stock was priced at 48, a country mile from the strike price. There was no reason to run the simulator, for the probability of hitting 7.50 would have been 0.

However, a word of caution here. When an option is extremely overpriced or extremely underpriced, there is probably a reason. In fact, ironically, buying and selling stocks based on this premise can be a profitable venture.

Here there was a reason; Cell Pathways, a drug company, had a drug that was coming up for FDA review. However, after a review of the price chart for CLPA, I found a lot of support at 10, and I probably would abort or get out with a small loss if it hit 10.

The worst case scenario would be that I would get the stock for a price of 6.50. (The put buyer has the right to put the stock to the writer at 7.50, but I already had 1 point in my pocket, so my cost is 6.50.) Even if CLPA were to go bankrupt without letting me out of the position, an unlikely scenario, my maximum loss would be 6.50. Here, I thought I had found a slam dunk play.

The extremely overpriced puts were a good signal that the stock would decline, and it did down to 15 from 48, but that still was far from the strike price of the puts that I had written. I had an easy win as I predicted.

You see, the option writers who write out-of-the-money options have two factors going for them: *time* and *distance*. To get writers in trouble, the underlying price must move against them fast enough to beat the expiration date and far enough to hit their stop-loss or strike price, sometimes an almost impossible task.

45

TIME—THE SECOND SECRET FOR OPTION WRITERS

You probably have already discovered the second secret: *time*. Only write options that have a small amount of *time* before they expire. If you remember, you should never hold options in the last month before expiration. For the writer, write options that have less than one month before expiration.

Avoid writing options that have more than two months before expiration. Option premiums collapse during the last month to the advantage of the writer. Your goal as a writer is to stay in an option position as short a period of time as possible. The more time you give the position, the more chance you have to get bitten.

Secret

46

GET OUT OF THE HOT SEAT!

Whenever I am in an option writing position, I consider myself to be in the *hot seat*, and my goal is to get out of the hot seat as quickly as possible. Consequently, I write out-of-the-money options that have little time left before they expire and that I will buy back immediately when they lose most of their value.

You don't want to be in an option position that is almost worthless and then surprise volatility comes along and the underlying stock, index or futures jumps into-the-money, hurting you big time (i.e. Twin Towers disaster). I also don't want to be in the hot seat when I see a major change in the underlying stock, index, futures or overall market.

Even where my stop-loss has not been hit, if I see a major

change in markets or the underlying security where it is moving against my position in a scenario I didn't plan for, I will exit immediately and get out of the hot seat!

When you are writing naked options or high risk credit spreads and when most of the premium has been captured or disappeared, you MUST EXIT your position. As a writer, you are in the HOT SEAT, and while in the hot seat, you are always in danger. Surprise volatility can bite you at any time. As a result, it is imperative that you always check your portfolio to see if you have option writing positions that have lost most of their value, and if they have, then act accordingly; as soon as you find an opening, get out!

The hot seat concept also applies to option buying when you have a profit. Preserving a big profit puts you in the hot seat. Don't let the profit slip away. When the underlying stock or futures stalls or reverses trend, get out of the the hot seat. Take the money and run.

47

EXPIRATION WRITING

One play that can generate almost sure wins is to write options that will expire in just a few days. (You still want to write options that are comfortably out-of-the-money.)

After I taught an old friend Frank (he had made millions in the stock market over the years) to trade options, he fell in love with the options game; he usually writes only naked put options with the intent of buying the stock, a concept we will cover in a later chapter. However, if he can find a buyer, he, too, likes to write expiring put options.

Now why would someone want to buy an option that is about to expire and has little chance of paying off? The key is that he is buying these options to close a position due to a margin call or to free some capital. What Frank does is put in a lot of option writing orders and position his limit price above the present bid price in the book. Then the next buy order will go to him.

Two examples may help. When Honeywell's merger with General Electric fell through, Honeywell dropped to 37. With one day before expiration, the HON Aug 30 put had a bid of .3 and an asked of .8. Frank put in an order to sell 10 HON Aug 30 puts at .40 ($40), and at the end of Thursday's trading, the order was filled. This is a 99% play. Honeywell would have to drop 7 points in one day after already hitting a temporary bottom before Frank could lose.

Of course, Frank pocketed the money. In the next expiration month of September, he did the same thing and put in an order to sell 10 Pfizer (PFE) Sept 30 puts at .10 ($10) when Pfizer was at 35. Someone bit at the order and bought the options at .10 with only a few hours before expiration. You could say that the $100 he received for writing the ten options was not much, but that is a free $100, the closest you will ever get to a sure thing.

To be successful at this play, you have to have a lot of patience and put in a lot of orders in the last two or three days before expiration.

One word of caution, one danger with all naked writing plays with stocks is that they have surprise volatility and can move in a chaotic pattern, so there are no absolute sure things.

48

DEFENSE, DEFENSE, DEFENSE

Whenever you are writing options, especially naked options, you must always be considering the worst case scenario. When you write options, you win quite frequently and, as a result, tend to relax when you should be in a disaster mode all the time, for all you need is one bad hit to wipe you out. Always ask yourself, "What is the worst thing that can happen to the position? Can I handle it? What can go wrong?"

Here are ten defensive steps that I take to protect my portfolio from a disastrous hit:

1. Use stop-losses.
2. Enter only high probability trades.
3. Write only short term options.

4. Write only overvalued options.
5. Cover positions when the option loses most of the value.
6. Never be afraid to take a loss.
7. Take small positions.
8. Exit a position when you feel uncomfortable.
9. Exit a position when the underlying scenario or trend changes.
10. Diversify.

The two most important steps to follow are the use of a stop-loss and taking small positions. Without a stop-loss, the option writer is doomed. Small positions will prevent you from taking a hit that will wipe out your portfolio. Remember you want to be able to return to fight another day!

49
WHEN TO USE COVERED CALL WRITING

One conservative way to write options is to do covered call writing. This is a way to generate additional income for your stock portfolio. Covered call writing refers to writing calls against the stocks that you own.

Here, there is no risk from writing the call. The obligation of writing the call is offset by owning the stock. For example, if you own 100 shares of Pfizer priced at 40 and write the Pfizer Jan 45 call at 2, you receive $200 to your account but are obligated if Pfizer is above 45 and you are exercised to deliver the stock at 45.

Covered call writing is ideal when you have a target where you wish to sell the stock. Then you are getting paid as you wait for the stock to hit your target. In our Pfizer example, if your target for Pfizer was 45, you receive $200 as you wait for the stock to exceed 45. If the stock does not get to 45, you can write another option with a strike price of 45 and collect more premium as you wait. If the stock is called away at 45, you receive 45+2 or $47 a share.

When you don't want to sell the stock, follow the guidelines that we presented in the previous chapters. Only write an out-of-the-money option with a high probability of expiring, set a stop-loss and buy back the option if the stop is hit. Then you can roll into a new option writing position, further out-of-the-money if you desire.

Your danger here is that the stock could gap up over the strike price, and you could take a bath buying back those options. Always close out all positions when most of the premium vanishes. Avoid covered call writing on a stock in a strong up-trend unless you believe it is making a top, and then it may be wiser to sell the stock than to write calls on the stock.

50

THE HIDDEN RISK OF COVERED CALL WRITING

Covered call writing is an extremely popular form of option writing, but there is a hidden disadvantage. When you write (sell) a call against a stock that you own, you are capping the profit or upside gain, yet you still have all the downside risk. That is why it is so important to roll out of a call position if the stock price moves across the strike price. Your stop-loss should always be set very close to the strike price.

Also, writing a covered call will not protect your downside. It may offset a point or two of loss, but not much more. If your stock position looks vulnerable, sell the stock or do a collar (sell a call and buy a put); don't write covered calls. Some studies suggest that in the longer term, call writing does not increase your returns, but does neutralize some of the short term risk and volatility of your portfolio.

51
COVERED CALL WRITING STRATEGIES

One covered call writing strategy that can generate much better returns is to write calls on low priced stocks, priced under $15 a share. Here you can sometimes find an overpriced call whose premium is a much higher percentage of the stock. Premiums on calls on lower priced stocks are much higher than premiums on high priced stocks.

However, don't buy a low priced stock just to write a high priced call against it. Make sure it is a stock that you want to own, or else you will own a bunch of dogs in your portfolio and your option premiums will not offset your losses from those stocks.

Sometimes you can create some really attractive risk-reward

plays by doing such covered writing. For example, in 2001, I bought 100 shares of Rambus at 16 and sold a Jan 2003, 25 call at 8. The premium paid for 50% of the stock (16 − 8 = 8), so my total cost and risk on the position was only 8. At the same time, I did not limit much of my upside profit. My potential profit is 25 less the cost of the stock at 8 or 17 points, which is over a 200% return.

52

USE NAKED PUT WRITING TO BUY STOCK

Naked put writing can be as conservative as covered call writing, for naked put writing is a way to buy stocks or futures. You see, the put writer is obligated to be "put" or to purchase the stock at the strike price.

Naked put writing is not popular with some option experts, but I believe it is an excellent way to try to buy stock at lower prices, and there are some experts that agree. Put writing is used by some of the big name investors like Warren Buffet and by corporations to buy back their stock.

Because the average investor has a tendency to buy stock at higher prices than desirable, naked puts have a particular advantage. When you write naked puts, you are forced to buy stock at lower prices.

Even though I am an aggressive put writer and follow all the rules I have laid out in previous chapters, such as buying back puts when they hit my stop-loss, I only write puts on stocks that I don't mind owning at the strike price.

Also, when I write naked puts, I only use mental stops so if the stock gaps below the strike price (remember—surprise volatility!), I have the option of buying the stock instead of taking a big loss on the put position if I have to buy back the option.

One warning here, make sure you have enough capital to buy the stocks that you write puts on.

53

NAKED PUT WRITING CAN CREATE A WIN-WIN STRATEGY

A win-win game situation is when you win regardless of what happens. Let's take an example to show how *win-win* put writing works. If Pfizer is at 40 and you want to buy the stock if it falls to 35, rather than placing a limit order to buy the stock at 35, write a Jan 35 put at 2 ($200).

Now if Pfizer is at or below 35 at expiration or if you are assigned before then (not too likely), you will buy the stock at 35, just what you wanted, but you already have $200 in your pocket from writing the put. Therefore. you actually only paid $33 a share.

Altogether, we have a win-win situation where you get Pfizer at $33 a share, which is exactly what you wanted, or if Pfizer is not below 35, you get a consolation prize—the $200 you collected. What if Pfizer drops to 30? Well, you were planning on buying the stock at 35 anyway. Here you are $200 richer.

Put writing is not appropriate when you want to buy a stock right away to take advantage of an immediate pending move. Put writing is best when you are trying to buy stock or futures at lower prices.

Sometimes you can generate a lot of income trying to buy a stock. One of my targets for put writing is a stock that is a takeover. If a major corporation decides to buy a company, it must think that company has a good value and the takeover company's puts are usually overvalued because of arbitrage activities. However, I only write puts on such stocks at strike prices at a point where they have long term support in the charts.

One good example of this strategy was when Monsanto was going to buy Delta Land and Pine (DLP). The takeover process took a long time and then fell through, but during that time I wrote a large number of different put positions and collected a lot of premiums. When the deal fell apart, DLP gapped down to 17 and I got the stock at 20. A few months later I sold the stock for 28, an 8 point profit. Here was a true win-win situation.

My friend Frank loves to write naked puts to buy stock, but

he uses a different ploy than I do. While I am writing shorter term puts to capture immediate income, he is writing longer term puts. These puts are way out-of-the-money on blue chip stocks that he loves. For Frank, put writing is a win-win game. Either he gets the option premium, or he gets his favorite stocks at much lower prices.

Section 5
Option Analysis

Secret

54

KNOW THE *TRUE VALUE* ADVANTAGE

The one thing I love about options over other investments is that you can measure their value and the probability of profit mathematically. That is not true of any other investments.

How do you measure the *true value* of a stock? There is too much uncertainty in the future to do so, and the fact that stock prices are all over the map each year demonstrates my point. How do you evaluate the true value of your home or of gold or silver or commodities, such as crude oil, corn and soybeans? We all try to guess at their value, but no one knows. Options, due to the fact they have a time limit and specific contract terms, can be measured mathematically.

There are several models that can be used for this purpose.

One such model, the Black and Scholes model, won a Nobel prize in Economics in 1997. Being that options are a surrogate for their underlying instruments, the models are based on the cost of holding the underlying security or futures. Even if you can't predict what the underlying securities and futures will do, having these models at your side, you can develop strategies that will show long term profits. Your goal is mathematically to identify underpriced or overpriced situations and to pounce on such opportunities.

Although most professionals mathematically analyze option plays, most investors do not. I am always in search of that super play on an over or undervalued option with an excellent risk-reward picture. That is what successful option trading is all about.

THE COMPUTER CAN DISCLOSE THE TRUE VALUE OF AN OPTION.

55

OPTION ANALYSIS CAN BE EASY

Every option investor should do some options analysis before entering a trade, but you do not need to be a math genius to do so. There are many option analysis software programs that enable you to do your option analysis easily.

Of course, some software programs are quite complex, and you can easily be lost in the trees. The secret is to keep things as simple as possible.

Here are the factors to look at before entering a trade:

1. What is the fair value of the option? Make sure you buy undervalued and sell overvalued.
2. What is your probability of profit if you hold the position to expiration?

3. What is your probability of hitting a stop-loss or profit goal during the life of the option? Here you will need a simulator.

4. What is the delta? If you are an option buyer, you want a higher delta. If you are an option writer, you want a lower delta.

These four factors are all you need to compare different option trades to determine the best play or if you should pass on a trade. A program like *Option Master*® will do all four tasks easily.

With this information, I can make my decision, and if I cannot get a statistical advantage in a trade where I have an under or overvalued situation or a good risk-reward picture, I pass on the trade. You need to gain an advantage in the markets. If you cannot get that advantage, pass on the trade.

**VOLATILITY IS THE KEY TO DETERMINING
THE FAIR VALUE OF AN OPTION**

56

THE KEY TO OPTIONS ANALYSIS

When you are trying to measure the fair value of an option and your probability of profit, there is one intangible factor that must be determined: the underlying security or futures *volatility*. What will the volatility be in the future? The volatility is a measure of how much the stock price or futures price will fluctuate or move up and down.

Many computer programs will require this historical volatility or calculate it for you. The historical volatility or statistical volatility is a standard deviation of change in price over a set period of days and weeks.

Professionals on the floor of the exchanges use a very short term volatility of between 20 and 30 days due to the fact they hold positions for very short periods of time, sometimes as little as a few hours to a few minutes. If you plan to hold option positions for longer periods of time, you should use a longer term historical volatility (i.e. 100 days or 20 weeks).

Historical volatilities are available on the web in a variety of locations, such as *ivolatility.com* . Once you have a good historical volatility, it is easy to measure the fair value of an option.

57

IMPLIED VOLATILITY— AN OPTION ANALYSIS SHORTCUT

Implied volatility is the volatility built into the option price. It is what the market thinks the volatility should be.

A computer program can measure the implied volatility by using the present option price and the pricing model, testing and retesting until the statistical volatility generates the present option price. That volatility, then, is the implied volatility; the implied volatility will usually come close to matching the historical volatility, suggesting the option is fairly valued.

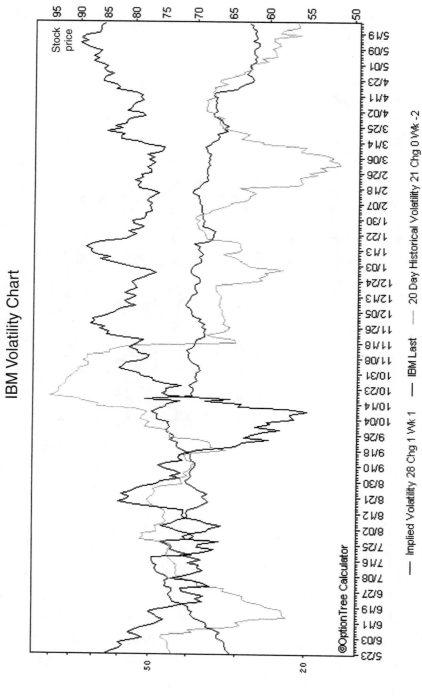

IBM Volatility Chart

Stock price

©OptionTree Calculator

— Implied Volatility 28 Chg 1 Wk 1   — IBM Last   — 20 Day Historical Volatility 21 Chg 0 Wk -2

The implied volatility is another way to determine if an option is over or underpriced. Look at a chart of the implied volatility for a stock or futures. (Check the IBM chart.) When the implied volatility is extremely low, based on its past history, the underlying option is underpriced. When the implied volatility is extremely high, based on its past history, the underlying option is overpriced.

The same procedure can be followed by looking at a chart of the historical volatility over the past months or years. Also, implied volatility can be used when calculating a probability of profit or or when using a simulator.

58

KEEP YOUR EYES ON THE DELTA

The delta is one of the Greeks (ratios) generated by pricing programs. The other Greeks are the gamma, theta, and vega. I rarely use the other Greeks, although they are used in scanner programs. To keep things simple, it is best to concentrate on the delta and avoid getting lost in the statistics of the other Greeks.

The delta is a measure of how much bang you will get for your buck if you are an option buyer. The delta tells you what percent an option price will move if the underlying security or futures moves 1 point.

For example, if the delta is .5, the option will move half a point if the underlying instrument moves 1 point. The delta is a good way to compare one option play to another; the higher the delta, the better the play for the option buyer; the lower the delta, the better the play for the option writer.

The delta is an excellent option analysis tool. Use it!

59

USE
PROBABILITY
ANALYSIS

Another tool that can help you find good opportunities is to calculate the probability of profit when you buy, write or enter an option spread. Since 1985, my computer program, *Option Master®*, has had a probability calculator. Now many others have added the feature.

The probability calculator enables you to determine the probability of making a profit if you hold the option positions until expiration in a random market. Similar to the delta, it is a good tool for comparing one option position to another. It is an excellent tool for spreads that are designed to be held till expiration.

Option buyers may be surprised at the results of the probability calculator, for your probability will never be greater than 50% in a random market and usually lower than most would think.

The point that should be made here is that we are assuming the position is held till expiration.

However, these low probability results demonstrate that you must be much more active as an option buyer and try to take action before expiration. The simulator discussed in the next chapter shows that much better probabilities can be attained if actions are taken during the life of the option.

60

THE SECRET WEAPON OF OPTION ANALYSIS

To beat the option game, you need to use the best technology available. Simulation is the closest thing to a crystal ball in the option markets. I have been using simulation since the 1970's and used it in my book, *The Option Player's Advanced Guidebook*. In the 1990's, I put my simulator in our *Option Master Software*. Since then, several other firms have started using simulation.

Simulation enables you to determine the probability of hitting a profit goal or stop-loss price based on the underlying security or futures. For example, if you planned to buy the January

Pfizer 45 call on October 15, when the stock is 41, what are the odds of hitting 47 by expiration? A simulator and probability calculator would tell you.

However, a simulator can also tell you the probability of hitting a stop-loss during the life of the option. Here, a regular probability calculator would not be as helpful, for it only tells you the probability if held till expiration, and with a stop-loss you need to know what happens during the life of the option. The stop-loss must be based on the underlying security or futures, for you are simulating the action of the underlying instrument.

The simulator in *Option Master*® also enables you to add a bullish or bearish bias to the simulation. Personally I would avoid that feature or enter a small bias, for as demonstrated in this book, we all have a difficult time predicting the future, and a high majority of us are usually wrong.

Altogether, I consider a simulator invaluable, for it gives you a much better view of whether you have a good or bad play, and, as a result, it gives you a big advantage in the option market. It also forces you to plan your trade before you enter it and to develop a game plan by setting profit goals and stop-losses. If the prediction from the simulator doesn't look good, pass on the trade.

61

A TOOL FOR YOUR ARSENAL

Another useful analysis tool for option buyers is a Percent to Double calculation. This feature of some software programs, including *Option Master® Deluxe*, is another way to compare one option buying position to another.

This tool tells you how much or what percent the underlying instrument has to move for the option to double in price. The smaller the number, the better the play for the option buyer, and the reverse would be true for the option writer.

However, the Percent to Double feature is a tool that should only be used for short term options.

62 SEARCHING FOR THE BEST PLAYS

Trying to find undervalued or overvalued option positions, or the best spread or best straddle can be a tedious task. What you need is a good scanning program. The top of the line programs, such as *Optionvue,* have good scanning features, but the web has provided an excellent alternative to software scanning programs that rely on your computer. Here you do not have the problem and headaches of downloading data to your computer. The data is accessed on the web.

Two web based programs that do such scanning are the *Power Analyzer* and *Option Research Scanner,* both available at *options-inc.com*. Both of these web-based scanning programs include volatility charts that were previously discussed. In the future, many other web-based scanning programs will probably be available.

Even though scanning for opportunities looks like an easy process, there is work to be done. Once you get a list of the most undervalued or overvalued plays, the work begins. In my newsletter, over 17 years I would run scans before every issue, but that was the easy part. Sorting through the list of best plays took a lot of time.

Out of a list of a hundred candidates, finding a few good plays was difficult. Even with carefully selected criteria, I would still get a lot of garbage—unfeasible plays. Also, when options are extremely overvalued or undervalued, you must question why! Extremely undervalued options are probably on a stock that is involved in a takeover where the takeover price is preset.

As I indicated previously, options that are extremely over-priced are probably overpriced for a reason. Find out why! Sometimes the overpriced nature of these options may predict future moves in the underlying security or futures. In other words, someone knows something you do not know. Nevertheless, scanning is still the best method to finding opportunities that will give you that statistical advantage in the options markets.

And this is just part of the process of doing your homework!

Secret

63

SITUATIONAL ANALYSIS

Another method that I use for finding option plays is situational analysis. I try to seek out specific stocks with an angle that may provide an interesting option play.

For example, on September 24, 2001, a negative news item on Electronics Data Systems (EDS) about incorrect financial reporting prompted me to take a close look at both the chart of EDS and its options. I found the options to be overpriced, and the chart showed that the stock price had a lot of resistance at 65. With the stock at 57, the Oct 65 call was .80 ($80) with only three weeks until expiration. Setting a stop-loss at 66, I ran a simulation of the probability of hitting the stop-loss. The simulator indicated only a 5% chance of hitting the stop-loss, and that is how it worked out. The play was to write the Oct 65 call naked, and the option expired with the stock never getting close to the stop-loss.

However, with news event plays, you must act immediately before the stock makes much of a move.

In my situational analysis all pieces must be in place. In this case here are the pieces: stock is likely to go down for the strategy's time span, options are overpriced, there is a high probability of winning, and it is a good looking chart, which here means a lot of overhead resistance.

When you find such a good statistical play, pounce on it, but don't plunge. Remember always take small positions when writing naked.

64

UNRAVELING THE MYSTERIES OF BAYSIAN ANALYSIS

When you have a good *feel* for the future price action of the underlying stock, you must convert that *feeling* into some concrete figures that will tell you which option strategy to select in order to be profitable in the options game. To do this, a short course on probabilities and probability theory is necessary. Don't panic. We'll make it an easy course, and ultimately the mysteries of the Baysian Analysis will be unraveled.

First, we're going to look at the area called *subjective probabilities*, which really means a good guess on the odds of something happening based on your intuition, knowledge and past experiences.

For instance, when you decide on the probability that the Green Bay Packers will beat the New Orleans Saints or the chances of having a thunderstorm this afternoon, you are using *subjective probability*. You are saying to yourself, "Well, given what I know about the situation, I *feel* there is a 70% chance that I'm going to need an umbrella today."

Baysian Analysis converts intuitive feelings into concrete numbers. For example, if you feel that an IBM July 60 call option for 3 ($300) with three months left in its life will be profitable because you feel the IBM stock price will move upward, how do you convert that into hard numbers?

First, let us establish a game plan where we will hold the IBM July 60 call option until expiration. Using technical analysis, combined with an ongoing analysis of the IBM fundamentals and plenty of homework on the other aspects of the market, we decide there is a 10% chance that IBM will be at 70 at the end of July, a 20% chance it will be at 65, a 40% chance it will be at 63, and a 30% chance that IBM will not be above 60 when the call option expires.

How did we come up with these probabilities? In a sense they were taken out of the air. Hopefully good homework on your part will make these probabilities more than just guesswork. The whole theory is based on taking your intuitive feeling, homework, and analysis and putting them down on paper.

How do we use these subjective probabilities to identify the profitability of our strategy? Let's add one more feature in mapping out this strategy. The profit or loss at each price level of the stock is as follows:

IBM Stock Price When Option Expires	Probability	Profit or Loss
70	10%	+$700
65	20%	+$200
63	40%	0
Below 60	30%	(-$300)

Note: Commissions not included.

Now we are ready to gaze into the crystal ball and find what the future holds. To do this, we will refer to the Baysian Decision Rule. This rule will provide our answer to the future. Rather than scare you with the formula, let's walk through this procedure in a nice and easy fashion.

First, let's take the 30% probability of losing all of our investment and multiply it times the $300 loss: ($300) Loss x 30% Probability IBM is at or below 60 when option expires = ($90) Loss.

Now let's do the same with all the other probabilities and profits or losses at each stock price level:

When IBM Stock Price is at 63:

$$\begin{array}{r} 0 \quad \text{Profit or Loss} \\ \times\ 40\ \% \\ \hline 0 \end{array}$$

When IBM Stock Price is at 65:

$200   Profit

$\underline{\times\ 20\ \%}$

$40

When IBM Stock Price is at 70:

$700   Profit

$\underline{\times\ 10\ \%}$

$70

Now let's add up all the results of these multiplications:

- − 90 ....IBM at 60 or lower
-   0 ....IBM at 63
- + 40 ....IBM at 65
- + 70 ....IBM at 70

+ $20 Profit or Loss (Expected Value)

The result of this multiplication and addition process is called our *Expected Value*—in layman's terms, our potential profit or loss. The profit or loss is the average profit or loss if we were to enter the same exact strategy thousands of times and determine the average return. In our example, the return on average would be $20 in the long run for a $300 investment, and let's emphasize THE LONG RUN.

Now you have a clear picture of the profitability of the strategy that initially looked pretty lucrative. Once you laid it out on paper and applied the Baysian Decision Rule, however, your long run profitability looks very thin.

This procedure, which takes only a few minutes to complete, can give you an invaluable glance at the future. Again, remember the *subjective probability* must be developed through your own analysis of potential stock prices.

In order to be successful using subjective probability, you have to take a realistic look at the stock or futures price action and not let emotion and enthusiasm for the stock or futures cloud your judgment. Now with a probability calculator and a simulator, you can get much more concrete numbers to carry out this analysis.

Altogether, the mysteries of Baysian Analysis have, I hope, been unraveled, and you can find its magic helpful.

65

GONE IN 60 MINUTES

How do you select options analysis software? When it comes to selecting options analysis software, you truly can get lost in the trees. Many programs on option analysis overkill. They are so complex and have so many features that you don't know where to start. Their complexity takes two weeks to learn, if you ever do, and one week to forget.

This is also the problem with most computer software—too much complexity, too difficult to learn and too easy to forget. Due to the complexity of options, you want to keep things simple!

A good rule to follow is if you can't learn how to use the software in 60 minutes, don't use it. In other words, try to select option analysis software that is really easy to use. All it has to do is complete the four or five tasks listed in this section of the book. If the software is too complex, you will quit using it. If it's easy, you will always use it. I can't tell you how many complex software programs I have on my office shelves that I stopped using.

When it comes to software, keep it simple or you will never use it.

66

AI—YOUR CRYSTAL BALL TO THE FUTURE OR RISK-REWARD ANALYSIS USING AI

With the rapid advancement in computer technology, Artificial Intelligence will play a more important role in options analysis in the future. Already there are computer programs that use AI to predict stock futures and price action (as we previously mentioned).

We developed two programs that use AI to evaluate the risk-reward picture of an option purchase (*The Push-Button Option*

Table I
The Push-Button Option Trader

OPTION PROFIT BOX®   05-30-2003
Upside Worksheet

** OPENING ACTION **
1. Buy TEXAS INSTRUMENTS (TXN) Oct 22.5-CALL Options at 1.3 (or in entry zone)
2. After entry, place a 'Good Til Canceled' order to sell the options at 2.3

** SURVEILLANCE ACTION **
3. Once in the position, daily plot the closing price of the underlying common
   stock in the Option Profit Box® below:

STOCK PRICE	(OPTION) PRICE		Implied Volatility: 40.8%
22.6	(2.3)		Delta: .404
22.0	(2.0)		
21.5	(1.8)		
21.0	(1.5)		
20.5	(1.3)	Entry Zone	
20.0	(1.1)		
19.5	(0.9)		

1 2 3 4 5 6 7 8 9 10 11 12 13 14 15
Trading Days After Recommendation

Prob of Upside Exit: 25%   Expected Value: $5.8
Prob of Downside Exit: 48%   Rating: 100

** CLOSING ACTION **
After you enter an Option Profit Box®, one of three possibilities can occur.
The daily plot of the underlying common stock can exit the Box at the TOP,
RIGHT SIDE, or BOTTOM. Your action and the end result of the trade is
detailed here:

    4. TOP Exit - This is the intended closing action and will trigger the
       GTC order you placed in #2 above.
    5. RIGHT SIDE Exit - The time has expired in the trade. SELL the options.
       Be sure to cancel the GTC order entered in #2 above.
    6. BOTTOM Exit - This requires stop-loss action on your part. SELL
       the options at the market price the following trading day. Be sure to
       cancel the GTC order you entered in #2 above.

** RECORD OF TRANSACTION **

	Date	Quantity	Price	Dollars (Net)
Opening				
Closing				
				Profit (Loss)

Table II
The Push-Button Option Writer

OPTION PROFIT BOX®
Upside Worksheet

05-29-2003

** OPENING ACTION **
1. Sell S & P 100 (OEX) Jun 510-CALL Options at 1 (Stock Priced at 482)
2. After entry, buy back the options if the stock hits the stop-loss of 511

** SURVEILLANCE ACTION **
3. Once in the position, plot the closing price of the underlying common stock
   in the Option Profit Box® below:

```
STOCK   (OPTION)                        Implied Volatility: 17.8%
PRICE    PRICE                          Delta: .102    Theta: .085
511.0  ( 9.4)

501.4  ( 5.2)

491.7  ( 2.5)

482.1  ( 1.0)

472.4  ( 0.3)

462.8  ( 0.1)

453.2  ( 0.0)
              1  2  3  4  5  6  7  8  9  10 11 12 13 14 15
                 Trading Weeks After Recommendation
```

Prob of Upside Exit: 7%   Expected Value: $34.2
Annualzed Return: 497%   Rating: 198

** CLOSING ACTION **
After you enter an Option Profit Box®, one of two possibilities can occur.
The plot of the underlying common stock can exit the Box at the RIGHT SIDE
or TOP (stop-loss). Your action and the end result of the trade is detailed
here:

   4. RIGHT SIDE Exit - The time has expired in the trade.
   5. TOP Exit - This requires stop-loss action on your part. BUY BACK
      the options at the market price.

** RECORD OF TRANSACTION **

	Date	Quantity	Price	Dollars (Net)	
Opening					
Closing					
					Profit (Loss)

Trader) and the risk-reward picture of an option writing position (*The Push-Button Option Writer*). AI makes options analysis easy for the option trader by giving him or her a method to rate the play, plus Expected Value generated by Baysian Analysis, discussed in Secret #64. A computer display of each program is shown in Table I and Table II.

The program automatically creates a game plan and, based on that game plan, is able to analyze the position automatically using option analysis tools we have discussed. Though the option investor can get instant analysis with little work on his part, these programs are unique because they only look at the risk-reward picture, rather than an undervalued or overvalued situation. Regardless, this is another form of option analysis that may be helpful.

Section 6
Spreading

Secret

67

THE SPREAD ADVANTAGE

Option spreading is another unique advantage of the option markets. Option spreads enable you to create strategies where you limit your risks and maximize your gains. Spreads allow you to adjust your positions as the market changes to neutralize market risks. Credit spreads, debit spreads, straddles, stripes and straps are all types of option spreads.

A well designed spread is one with an excellent risk-reward picture. For the option buyer, spreads are, to use baseball jargon, for those who are satisfied with singles and doubles instead of home runs. For the option writer, spreads can remove the unlimited risk present with naked writing. The big advantage of spreads is that spreads can be designed with a high probability of profit and very limited risk. (At the end of the book, we will disclose two of the best plays in the option markets, spreads with these features.)

A spread is best defined as a combination of buying and selling (writing) two or more different options at the same time usually on the same underlying issue. Any professional option trader should know how to spread and use it as a tool and as part of his option trading arsenal. The difficult part of spreading is learning how to design a spread and understand the risk-reward picture for the spread, which takes some practice.

Secret

68

THE SECRET COSTS OF OPTION SPREADS BEWARE OF SLIPPAGE!

One of my major rules of successful option trading is to minimize your trading. There are high costs to option trading. Not only are there commissions, but also there is slippage—the distance between the bid and asked price. And that slippage can be quite large, sometimes a large percentage of the option price. That is a real cost.

Hence, when you trade spreads, you magnify that cost. Just a simple spread will usually involve four trades—two trades to get in and two trades to get out. Add to this the complexity and difficulty of getting in and out of spreads, and you can see the challenge you face. Such obstacles mean only one thing when you are spreading: keep it simple!

BEWARE OF ALLIGATOR SPREADS FOR THE COMMISSIONS
AND SLIPPAGE CAN EAT YOU ALIVE!

Secret

69

BEWARE OF ALLIGATOR SPREADS

With the high costs and difficulty of trading spreads, when you write complex spreads, such as butterfly spreads, which involve three trades in and three trades out, you are in deep trouble. As a result, whenever anyone mentions such spreads, I am turned off. In the business we call such spreads, *alligator spreads*, for the commissions and slippage will eat you alive.

Alligator spreads look great on paper but rarely work out in actual trading. Avoid any spread that involves three trades to get in the position, for if you don't, you will become a prey of the alligator.

Secret

70

AVOID DELTA NEUTRAL STRATEGIES

Delta Neutral strategies have received a lot of hype over the last few years. They involve putting on a spread by adding and subtracting legs as the market moves. You do this to keep your market position neutral so that you profit no matter what the market does.

On paper this strategy looks great, but in practice it rarely works well. The problem you face is too many trades. I can't overemphasize how important it is to minimize your trading, or the alligator will get you. Whenever you are planning a strategy, keep it simple.

71

AVOID REPAIR STRATEGIES

When a trade goes bad, many experienced option traders use repair strategies. They will add an option leg to protect a position or use a variety of other option strategies to avoid taking a loss.

There are some situations where repair strategies buy you some time for the position to move in your favor, but in many cases the trader just does not want to take a loss, and all the repair strategy does is increase his or her trading activity—a game that you want to avoid.

One of the greatest errors made by an option trader is his inability to take a loss. This means that when your option trade goes astray, cut your losses! Don't use a repair strategy.

72

HOW TO REDUCE THE COST OF OPTION BUYING

Spreading is an excellent way to reduce the cost of an option purchase. This spread is usually called a *debit spread*. To design the spread, you buy one option and write another option against that position, either at a different strike price (a *vertical spread*) or expiration month (a *calendar spread*).

Vertical spreads work well for reducing the cost of the position but limit your profits so that you can't hit home runs. They work best when at-the-money options are less expensive in comparison to their out-of-the-money options. That can be measured by calculating the *implied volatility* of each option. For example, if the implied volatility of the option you are purchasing is 30%, but the out-of-the-money option you are writing has an implied volatility of 40%, you have a good play.

Here is how a spread works. If you bought the PFE Jan 40 call for 2, you could offset the cost of that option by writing or selling the PFE Jan 45 call for 1. Now the cost of your position is only 1 point instead of 2, but you cannot profit beyond 45.

Altogether, your risk-reward picture looks like this. You risk 1 point to make a 5 point gain (45-40=5), less the cost of the option you bought; your maximum profit is 4. Here you have a potential 400% return on your investment.

Running a probability analysis will also help you decide whether you have a good trade or not, and, as previously mentioned, measuring the implied volatility of both options will give you some valuable input. The beauty with these spreads is that you can not lose more than you paid for the spread, and that is also your margin requirement.

73

RULES OF
THE ROAD

I have established a series of rules for the road for designing debit spreads for stocks, indexes and commodities.

How to Design a Stock or Index Debit Spread

1. Buy a close-to-the-money option.
2. Sell a further out-of-the-money option.
3. The maximum profit must be at least 200%.
4. Do not sell an option for less than .4.
5. Try to design a spread with a probability of profit of 35% or better.

How to Design a Commodity Option Debit Spread

1. Buy a close-to-the-money option.
2. Sell a further out-of-the-money option more than one strike price out.
3. The maximum profit must be at least 300%.
4. Do not sell an option for less than $100.
5. Always use a spread order.
6. Try to design a spread with a probability of profit of 35% or better.
7. Never pay a commission of more than $20 round trip per side.

Spreading seems complex but can be simple if you keep it simple.

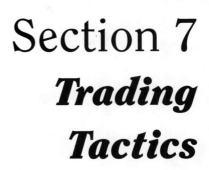

Section 7
Trading Tactics

74

GO ONLINE!

It is important that we gain every advantage we can in the market. One important trading tactic that has a big advantage over traditional trading is internet trading. Traditional trading, telephone trading, where you have to call a broker to execute a trade is too slow and hurts your agility in the market. Internet trading allows you to get immediate feedback regarding the status of a trade and allows you instantly to modify a trade as many times as you like without having to make any calls to a broker.

Another problem with a personal broker is that you will hesitate to call him to change a trade because you feel you will impose on his time. On the internet you have far more flexibility, and interpersonal relationships will not interfere with your decision-making process. You can enter, modify or cancel orders within a few minutes or seconds, and there are no barriers such as a broker or clogged phone lines to get in your way.

There is no question that the internet will give you an edge in the market by giving you better trade executions. That means better prices for the option trades. So go online!

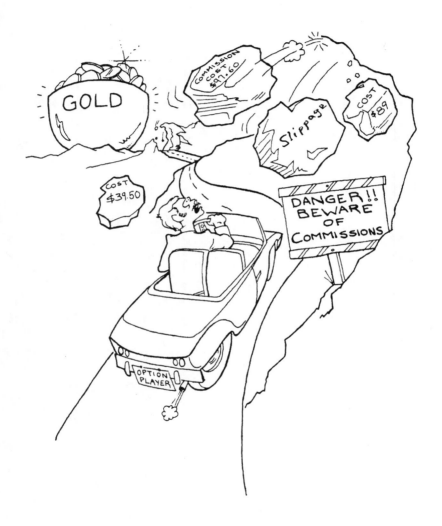

75

THE HIDDEN COST OF TRADING

When we talk about the cost of trading, we usually think of commissions, but there is an even greater cost of trading, and that is *slippage*. Slippage is the difference between the bid and asked price. The bid price is what you can sell the option for, and the asked price is the price you need to pay to buy the option. For example, if the bid and asked price on an option is 1 at 1.3, you can sell the option for 1, but must pay 1.3 to buy it.

With options, slippage can be a good percentage of the price of the option. In our example, .3 is the slippage, which can be as much as 30% of the price of the option. In casino parlance, there is the *take* along with the commissions, and in casinos, the *take* or house advantage on roulette is over 5%. It can be much higher when you are trading options due to slippage.

In conclusion, when you trade, you must do everything you can to reduce slippage. This means you must reduce the number of trades that you make because every trade that you make incurs a slippage cost. That is why I don't like complicated trades where you enter and exit too many positions. Also, when you trade cheaper options, slippage is higher because it is a much higher percentage of the option cost.

How do you reduce slippage? Keep it simple, minimize your trading and try to trade options with more liquidity, options with good volume that trade more often. Here the spread between the bid and asked price is not as wide.

In addition to slippage, commissions can sneak up on you and bite you, Option trading involves a lot of trades, so you must get the lowest commissions possible. If you do not, you will not survive.

If you are paying more than $5 per option in commissions, you are in real trouble. Try to avoid paying more than $3 per option. Go with brokerage firms that have a low minimum commission. There are many brokerage firms on the internet that offer low rates.

**TEST THE WATERS WITH LIMIT ORDERS
AND USE THE PRIORITY ADVANTAGE**

76

ACT LIKE A
MARKET
MAKER

One way to reduce or eliminate the cost of slippage is to act like a *market maker*. The market makers are usually behind most option trades. They usually sell at the asked and buy at the bid price. They are the players who make the market and pocket the slippage.

In options that don't trade much, they're the only players in the market, and they provide the bid and asked price. With the speed and instantaneous feedback of the internet and with much lower commissions charged on the net, you can act like a market maker.

As a public player, you have *priority* over the market makers' bid and asked prices. As a result, if you set your limit price to buy an option at the bid price and the only other player is the market maker, you will get your order filled before him.

The market maker does have other advantages, such as margin and low priced hedging vehicles, but if you are patient and quick at changing limit option prices as the underlying changes in price, you could get some excellent trade executions and pocket some of that slippage.

77

TEST THE WATERS— HOW TO GET THE BEST PRICE

There is one easy technique that you can follow to get better trade executions or better option prices when you buy or sell options. When you are determined to buy or sell an option, test the water first.

For example. you want to buy an option that is quoted 1 at 1.3. To buy that option right now, you will need to pay 1.3, the asked price. But take a minute or two to test the water. Enter a limit price of 1.15 and see if the market maker will bite. You will be surprised how many times you will get your price (i.e. 1.15) instead of the asked price of 1.3.

If your order at 1.15 is not filled after a few minutes, you can modify your order and pay the asked price by entering a market order or limit order at the asked price. Of course, the tactic probably will only work if you are trading online.

A postscript is necessary here. When you enter an order with your broker, his floor broker is suppose to work to get you the best price. However, honesty is not the best virtue on the floor, and floor brokers can tip off the market makers to what order they hold in their hands. Consequently, it is best to maintain control of your order and use the internet to negotiate your trade.

78

YOU CAN BUY THE WORLD FOR 1/8

"You can buy the world for 1/8." is an old Wall Street adage which means that investors will lose a major opportunity by not being willing to pay 1/8 of a point more to get their trades off.

Today stocks and stock options are not quoted in fractions anymore, but rather decimals, yet the same rule applies. Don't chase after option prices, but be willing to pay an extra .10 ($10) or .15 ($15) to enter a trade if you have a really good opportunity. In other words, be more flexible in trying to get a good price for your trade. In the past I have lost some good opportunities by being too inflexible in my trading.

Of course, there are times that you must get out of a position, especially if you are a naked writer. You can try to get a good price for a minute or two, but then you must pay whatever the market will bear.

79.
HOW TO ENTER SPREAD POSITIONS

Spreads can be great trades, but for most investors they are harder to execute. You should usually use spread limit orders to enter spread positions. Here, you specify the maximum price or *debit* you wish to pay for a *debit spread* and the minimum *credit* or price you wish to receive for a *credit spread*.

A *debit spread* is a trade where you pay a price to enter the spread, like buying options. A *credit spread* is a trade where you receive a premium price when you enter the trade, like writing or selling options.

For example, to enter a spread where you buy an IBM Oct 80

call at 3 and sell an IBM Oct 90 call at 1, you would enter a spread order. Forget about the prices of the options. Look at the differences (i.e. 3 − 1 = 2). Here, the difference is 2 points. The spread order would say to buy the IBM 80 and sell the IBM 90 for a debit of 2 points.

The problem with spread orders is that they can be hard to get executed even if the bid and asked prices are in the right place.

On the other hand, the big advantage of the spread order is that you don't risk losing control of the spread as you add each leg of it. Either you get the spread price you want, or you do not get the trade executed.

On several occasions I set a spread price where I was buying at the asked price and selling at the bid price, and though it was a trade that should have been executed automatically because it was a spread order, it wasn't. The good part is that I never had to worry about losing control if one or the other leg of the trades had gone through, leaving me naked.

80

SECRET SPREADING TACTICS

Even though I strongly suggest using spread orders to enter and exit spread positions, since the advent of the internet, I usually don't use spread orders but rather leg in and leg out of positions. In other words, I will execute one side of the spread first and then the other side. This practice ensures an execution of the spread and, if done right, usually at a better price than a spread order.

However, there is always the risk of losing control of the spread and taking a big loss. Therefore, legging into and out of a spread should be avoided in a fast moving market.

Nevertheless, with the speed and immediate feedback possible on the internet, such spreading tactics can work very well.

Here is how to enter such trades. Let's say that you want to enter an IBM debit spread where you buy IBM April 50 call priced at 2–2.5 and sell the IBM April 55 call priced at 1–1.25 Usually you enter the buy side of the trade first so you are not naked at any time. You first would enter an order to buy the IBM Apr. 50 call at 2.25. Give it a few minutes, and if the order has not been filled, move the limit to the asked price of 2.50. Enter the second order to sell the IBM Apr. 55 call. First enter an order to sell at 1.12 between 1 and 1.25, but then immediately change it to a market order.

Your danger, here, is that IBM might move against you before you can get the second leg of the trade off. So, again, avoid fast moving markets. Spread orders are always the safer way to go, but if you use spread orders, always use a limit order.

81

DON'T TIP YOUR HAND— BEWARE OF SIZE

A classic error made by many option players is that they enter too large an order, resulting in poor executions or fills.

Whenever you see an option quote such as 2 at 2.50, at that moment the asked price of 2.50 is guaranteed for 10 contracts and the bid price is guaranteed for 10 contracts. We call that "10 up on a side". (One exchange suggested that they were going to 20 up on a side.) If you enter a larger order, the market makers will adjust their bid and asked price against you.

As a result, try to avoid tipping your hand; enter orders of a maximum of 10 contracts at a time. Once one order is executed, you can enter another. Eventually the market makers will catch on to your play, but initially you will get better prices.

Section 8

Trading Tips

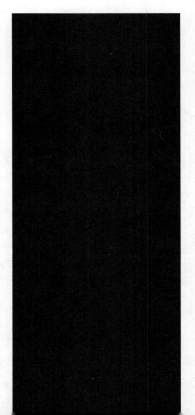

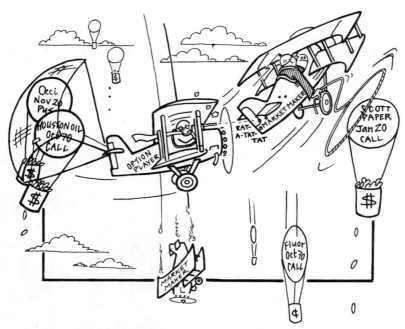

WHEN YOU ARE TRADING OPTIONS YOU ARE AT WAR!

82

THE TOP SECRET WAR ROOM

When I trade, I consider my trading office to be a war room, for when I trade, I am at war with the markets, market makers, the professional traders and the general investing public. In fact, on my desk is a letter opener labeled "Cabinet War Room", acquired when I visited the war room bunkers where Winston Churchill waged war against the Nazis. For when you trade, you are at war, and every ounce of energy should be applied to gaining an edge and locating your enemies.

One of your enemies is your own emotions. One way to keep them in control is to keep your attack plans top secret. Don't tell anyone what you are doing, including your wife or husband. As soon as you tell someone about your trades, you put pressure on yourself not to take a loss WHEN YOU SHOULD, for your ego is at stake.

One advantage of internet trading is that you don't have a personal broker to lead you either astray or threaten you with an "I told you so" attitude. Even good personal brokers will put pressure on you to perform when the trades are your own idea, even if they say nothing. Nevertheless, a good broker can be invaluable, especially if you're just starting to trade.

DON'T TRY TO CATCH A FALLING KNIFE!

Secret

83

DON'T TRY TO CATCH A FALLING KNIFE!

Other slogans that apply here are: "Don't stand under a falling grand piano," and "Don't stand in front of a runaway locomotive." The severe bear market of 2000–2002 taught many investors a painful lesson about trying to buy stocks that are in a major decline. Cheap stocks got a lot cheaper!

Naked writers should really take note here. You have extreme risk. If the underlying stock or futures starts to move against you, run for cover. Don't write puts in the face of a major downtrend. Don't buck strong momentum in the market.

84

ONLY PLAY WITH FUN MONEY

One of the classic statements in the options game is "Don't play with money you cannot afford to lose." This statement truly applies to option buying, especially shorter term options where the payoffs are few and far between.

In fact, I would be more emphatic here. Money you can afford to lose is still money that you value. You need to play with money that you are willing to light up with a match, money that is treated as worthless plastic poker chips on a table. Casinos make you use poker chips and tokens when you play slots or blackjack and roulette so you won't value them and be afraid to play more chips.

When you buy options, set aside some fun money every year

and kiss it good-bye. (Look how quickly many of you lost valuable money during the 2000–2002 bear market.) Why not pull out a small amount of capital each year to apply to games you can have a lot of fun at?

If you treat such money as *fun* money, you will be able to withstand losing streaks and be willing to continue to take positions until you hit the home runs. To be successful trading options, you cannot have a faint heart but must plow ahead and buy options month after month without quitting, knowing in the end you will show a profit. The only way you can do this is to use *fun* money.

Most investors fail at this endeavor, for they are not prepared to stay for the long haul and will quit after taking a few losses.

Secret

85

KNOW WHEN TO FOLD THEM!

Being afraid to take a loss is a classic error of the option player, especially option writers and spreaders.

When your trade goes bad, get out!

When you are uncomfortable in a position and can't sleep at night, get out!

When the trend of the underlying goes against you, get out!

Being able to bail out of positions is critical to your success; if you hesitate, you are lost! Remember, taking losses in option trading is a virtue, not a sin. When you are an option writer with high risks, exiting is your only *lifeline*, and when things go against you, use that lifeline and get out of that position even if you must take a loss. The secret to success when playing poker is to "know when to fold them". The same rule applies to option trading.

Secret

86

THE SECRET
OF SUNK
COST

As you now know, one of the most critical attributes of a successful option trader is his ability to take a loss. One major reason investors have trouble taking a loss is *sunk cost*. They reflect on how much they paid for that stock, futures or option, or how much they will lose.

What you paid for that stock or option should be considered a *sunk* cost and must be ignored in making an investment decision. The question becomes whether the stock or option is a good investment at today's price, ignoring what you paid previously.

Unfortunately, too many investors make this mistake of sunk cost by making their decisions based on the price they paid for a stock, futures or options when they should be asking themselves the question, "Would I buy at today's price?" Don't be one of those unfortunate investors. If you realistically would buy at today's price, then hang on to the position. If not, sell the position.

Here, I don't understand when an analyst gives a HOLD rating on a stock. Either a stock is worth buying or else you should sell it. Having a HOLD on a stock or futures says that you must hold on because you paid a higher price. That is bad decision-making, for you are considering your sunk cost.

Most people in every-day-life situations consider sunk costs when they should not. For example, let's say you have an old car or lemon and keep pouring money into fixing that car. Your excuse is that you have already invested too much money in the car to sell it; however, you will never get your money back, and furthermore, the more you pour in, the more you lose.

As a result, the refrain is that you should never consider what you have already invested; that is sunk cost, and you always ignore sunk cost. A good poker player never considers how much he has already put in the pot; he considers his chances of winning, not his investment in the pot. He knows when to fold his cards.

87

ALWAYS USE STOP-LOSSES, AND DON'T LOOK BACK

Whether you are buying options or writing options, stop-losses are an important lifeline to your success. Stop-losses are exit points where if the option or stock price is hit, you automatically exit the position.

Through many hours of system-back testing to trade stocks, we found stop-losses greatly improved the results of the system. *Stop-losses will prevent you from taking major losses and letting big profits slip away.* Stop-losses would have saved many investors from disaster during the most recent bear market.

Stop losses are a MUST for naked writers and credit spread traders. If you don't use them, you are doomed.

When entering stop-loss orders, I usually enter a contingency stop-loss, where I exit the option position if the underlying stock or futures hits the specified price. You can apply stop-losses using the option price, but make sure to use the option bid or asked price, not the last price because an option may not trade for a long time, a long time after the stock or futures has hit the stop-loss prices.

I prefer using the underlying stock or futures as the basis for a stop-loss, for option prices can do funny things. Your problem will be finding a broker who will allow contingency stop-loss orders. However, there are brokers that will allow such orders, so keep searching.

Another use of stop-losses is a trailing stop-loss. I usually use a mental stop-loss here. Such a stop-loss is used to prevent profits from slipping away. For example, if you have a call option with a big profit, keep adjusting the stop-loss as the stock or futures moves in your direction (i.e. keeping it 5% away from the stock or futures price). When it reverses course and touches your stop-loss, take profits.

Stop-loss orders are one of your most important lifelines, so use them!

Moreover, when a stop-loss kicks you out of a strategy or position or when you take a profit, don't look back and second guess yourself. Many times when you are *stopped* out of a position, you would have fared better if you had not used the stop. However, stops are designed to prevent disasters to your portfolio, and the one time you ignore a stop will be the time that does you in.

Always obey your stop-loss point, especially when it comes to option writing positions. If you hesitate and disobey that stop-loss one time, you probably shouldn't be playing this game. The statement, "If you hesitate, you are lost," surely applies. You must have the discipline to use and follow your stop-losses.

To repeat, when taking profits, don't look back. You may have fared better if you didn't take the profits, but Monday morning quarterbacking may result in losing a big profit in the future.

88

CHECK YOUR TRACK RECORD

Not Looking back does not mean not critiquing your past performances. As an option trader, your most important learning experience is to review your track record at least once a year. Such a review will disclose the mistakes that you made, and we all make mistakes. Here, you can alter trading tactics in order to avoid such mistakes in the future.

I strongly suggest that you write down a series of guidelines that you have established after looking at your past trades. These guidelines include being more aggressive about taking profits or changing where you set your stop-losses, and the list goes on. Check out your bad trades and find out what went wrong. An honest review of your past performances will surely pay off with improved performance in the future.

89

THE DRAGON THAT YOU SEE IS NOT THE DRAGON THAT WILL BURN YOU

The theme here is be prepared for the unexpected. The Twin Towers disaster is the perfect example of the unexpected. Here we come back to surprise volatility. Such volatility is the friend of the option buyer but the enemy of the option writer.

After numerous surprise bankruptcies of large corporations

in 2002, everyone is scared of the market, not knowing who to trust. In 1987 when the Dow gapped down 500 points, a big percentage at the time, many option writers were scared away forever, but the Dow didn't act like this again for a long time.

The dragon you think you see coming is probably not the dragon that will ultimately attack you! The next dragon to burn you probably will come from an unexpected corner of your investing kingdom. Consequently, the scared traders in 2002 most likely will not be looking in the right direction when the dragon attacks.

Options give you the advantage of reducing risks and surviving those devious dragons. Be prepared for the unexpected.

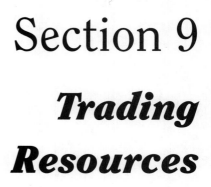

Section 9

Trading Resources

90

TREASURES
ON THE
INFORMATION
HIGHWAY

One of the major reasons to have access to the internet is due to the vast amount of resources available on the net. You have the largest library of information available at your finger-tips. That library keeps expanding every day by leaps and bounds, and most of it is free.

On the net you can research any stock in great detail. For example, *quicken.com* provides a very good fundamental analysis from several angles. Using search engines, such as Google, can quickly lead you to the specific information you are looking for. Web-based programs that will scan a large data base of stocks or options are a true breakthrough for the trader. The research you can do is only limited by your imagination!

The option game is a very competitive game, and, remember, you are at war with the rest of the option players. To gain the edge, you must do your homework, and that homework involves using the knowledge and tools available on the web.

9 1

AVOID ANALYSIS PARALYSIS

The mathematical nature of the options game in combination with the unpredictable nature of stocks and futures and vast resources of the internet can create a large trap for the option trader. Many traders suffer from information overload. They cannot decipher the good information from the bad information, and they get lost in the trees.

Many investors overanalyze to the point that they are unable to make a decision. Many technical analysts get lost in the jungle of statistics of the price charts. That is why there are so many different opinions about the same stock or futures price action.

Try to keep things simple. Stand on the sidelines instead of in the middle of the jungle. Take a lot of the information with a grain of salt. Remember my 60% rule in Secret #15. When it comes to option traders, decide on the important input and ignore the other details.

For example, concentrate on the delta, probability of hitting your target, implied and historical volatility, and theoretical value. Don't get lost when doing your analysis, and don't consider numbers to be printed in stone. Also, avoid using too many analysis programs and too many option advisory services. Too much information can be as dangerous as too little.

Try to keep it simple, and try to develop a simple consistent methodology that suits your personality and style. Of course, a simple methodology takes practice as you get comfortable with the type of trades and analysis that you find successful.

92

HOW TO USE OPTION ADVISORY SERVICES

Having written an option advisory newsletter as early as 1973, I have found the secrets of how to use and not use such services. Many investors who use such services think the services are a magic bullet, the guru that will lead them to the promised land. They quickly become severely disappointed. There is no magic bullet or road to quick fortunes out there. Only you can lead yourself to high profits.

Option advisory newsletters go out to hundreds and sometimes thousands of subscribers. Options have very limited liquidity, and when an option is recommended in an advisory newsletter, its price is highly impacted. You may have to pay more than you should for that option play. Or you may only get trades off when the underlying instrument moves in the wrong direction, and you will be stuck with a bunch of losing positions. The key to success in option trading is to stay away from the crowd, and when you use advisory recommendations, you are following a large crowd.

Option advisory services should be used as a guide to lead you to good plays. One of my favorite option newsletters is *The Option Strategist* by Larry MacMillan, but I have never used one of the newsletter's recommendations. I use the newsletter to give me ideas from which I create my own trades. One idea or angle can pay for many times the price of the service.

When using an option recommendation, counter the crowd. Use a different option on the same underlying instrument, or enter the position a few days later. Don't take profits at the recommended price. Take the profit before the price is hit. Set your stop-loss further out than the recommended price. Never use the parameters set by the newsletter. Try to outmaneuver the likely moves of the other subscribers. Remember, you are at war with the other players.

The option price is the most important aspect of any play or strategy. If you can't get your price, wait till you can or pass. Never chase after an option recommendation unless the option continues to be underpriced.

Only use option advisory recommendations that give you a statistical or mathematical advantage.

Secret

93

THE
5 P'S

If you don't know where you're going, you'll end up some place else."

—Yogi Berra

The 5 P's are Proper Planning Prevents Poor Performance, or plan before you play. Good management is an important part of option trading. Most investors enter the option game totally unorganized. They have unrealistic expectations and don't understand the risk-reward picture of the strategies they enter.

To be successful, you need a well defined game plan of each position you enter, written down in black and white (See Secrets #29 and #66), and an overall game plan or strategic plan. This plan, for example, would map out how many positions and what kind of trades you will enter each month and each year. If you are an option buyer, this is critical, for such a plan will force you to stay the course and not quit and stop buying options when you should be buying.

Such planning should lay out the maximum risks of the trade as well as the profit potential. In planning your trades, make sure each trade or strategy gives you a mathematical or statistical advantage or some kind of edge. Set some overall profit objectives, but make sure they are realistic.

If you do the proper options analysis, you will know how often you will be successful and you will have few surprises. A good battle plan is truly the only way to long term success in the options game.

Secret

94

THE MAGIC PYRAMID

Every investor should have a grand master plan. In other words, an asset allocation plan, a plan that shows how you will invest your liquid assets. The question is how should options fit into that plan.

Options enable you to have a much more hedged portfolio, much more cushioned from risk yet with the ability to generate much better gains than a traditional portfolio.

The Magic Pyramid lays out the grand master plan. At the base of the pyramid are your cash and cash equivalents (i.e. T-bills, money market funds, etc.). I am a big advocate of having a lot of cash. And with options you can greatly enlarge your cash holdings and use option strategies to provide the opportunity for growth to your portfolio.

One level above your cash position would be your bond holdings. Here, only include high rated short term and intermediate bonds, especially if rates are low. To cover some of the currency risk, an international bond fund may be wise. Swiss bonds are a good alternative here.

About 5% to 10% of your portfolio should be in hard assets, such as gold or platinum or securities that produce such assets.

The next level of your asset pyramid would be stocks or mutual funds. Here the structured products we discussed would be very appropriate. They allow equity participation with little downside risk, a risk that most investors have discovered is much higher than they had thought.

Options should be an important part of your stock portfolio. Put writing can be used to acquire stock at lower prices. Covered call writing can be used to take profits and generate more income for your portfolio. Buying cheap puts can provide a downside cushion of insurance and protection for your stock portfolio. Buying Leaps® and Leaps® spreads (to be covered in the next section) can be used as a surrogate for stocks to reduce the downsize risk and increase potential rewards. Altogether, options can maximize the gains and minimize the risks for your stock portfolio.

The next level of the pyramid is for more aggressive option strategies. Here debit spreads, credit spreads, diagonal spreads and ratio spreads would come into play, and for the gladiators in the crowd, naked writing.

At the peak of the pyramid, you need some option plays that will give you firing power for your portfolio. Here I would buy or build a portfolio of cheap options year after year, always going for the home runs. This is the part of the portfolio where your *fun* money comes into play, but never use more than 5%–10% of your portfolio to do so.

Section 10

Power Plays

95

"THAR IS GOLD IN THEM THAR HILLS"

From my research, experience and track record, I have found that the most powerful of all option strategies is to just BUY CHEAP OPTIONS, especially puts. We have discussed the inherent statistical advantage in buying options due to the fact that stock prices move in a chaotic pattern, sometimes far beyond the range of the pricing model's parameters.

Such surprise volatility makes options gems in the rough, or "gold in them thar hills". Buying cheap options, you truly have a mathematical and statistical edge, something you are looking for as you play the game.

However, finding the gold is more difficult than most people think. As mentioned previously, most cheap options are not good plays. They are overvalued with little chance of paying off. Therefore, it is important that you analyze an option before you buy it. You must know your probability of making a profit, the theoretical value of the option, the delta and implied volatility.

The best way to find these plays is to use a SCAN program that identifies undervalued options. We previously mentioned several excellent web-based programs that can do the job.

After I identify a list of undervalued options, I look at the charts of the underlying (i.e. check out *bigcharts.com*) to make sure the underlying stock or futures does not face a lot of overhead resistance for calls or underlying support for puts and also to see if the underlying security has made the necessary move in the past within the time frame allotted.

Then I look at a chart of the implied and historical volatility of the stock or futures (such charts are available in the Option Research Scanner and the Power Analyzer.) to make sure these volatilities are at a low ebb on the charts. Finally, I would do the probability analysis prescribed to ensure I am not betting on a dead horse.

Option buying should be part of every option investor's arsenal. It provides excellent insurance and explosive firing power for your portfolio.

The drawback here is that in practice, most investors do not fare well buying options. They do not have the patience, discipline and ability to handle a lot of losses.

96

RULES OF THE ROAD FOR OPTION BUYING

To help you in your option buying activities, I have established a series of guidelines for buying both stock and futures options. These rules of the road should help you pick out those winners.

Rules of the Road for Buying Stock Options

1. Buy only underpriced options.
2. Buy cheap options—options priced under 1 or under 2.5 for Leaps.

3. Buy close-to-the-money options.
4. Buy options with as much time as possible before expiration.
5. Buy options where the underlying stock has the potential for increased volatility in the future.
6. Put the same number of dollars in each position.
7. Diversify over time (2 years).
8. Buy in quantity to save commissions.
9. Buy an option where the stock price has a good chance to move across the strike price.
10. Try to buy options where there is at least a 20% chance of profit.

Rules of the Road for Buying Commodity Options

1. Buy only underpriced options.
2. Do not pay more than $400 for an option.
3. Buy close-to-the-money options.
4. Buy options with as much time as possible before expiration.
5. Buy options where the underlying commodity has the potential for increased volatility in the future.
6. Diversify over time (2 years).
7. Buy a commodity option where the underlying commodity price has a good chance to move across the strike price.
8. Try to buy options where there is at least a 20% chance of profit.

97

AGGRESSIVE WRITING WITH LIMITED RISK

A powerful play is the INDEX CREDIT SPREAD.

Naked writing has a big advantage over many other plays because you win almost all the time, but unlimited risks and sometimes margin requirements are too much for most investors to handle. In addition, when you write stock options naked, the surprise volatility puts you at a disadvantage and can bite you badly!

To counter the danger of surprise volatility, you could write broad-based index options on indexes, such as the S&P 500 Index. Here you don't have as much surprise volatility because the index neutralizes the volatility of individual stocks, but writing such options during the crash of 1987 resulted in financial disaster for thousands of investors.

There is an alternative that reduces the risk of such plays, and that is the *index credit spread*. Since the late 1980's, I have been recommending such trades in my newsletter, and these trades have generated an excellent track record.

Credit spreads limit your risk, greatly reduce your margin requirements, and, when designed properly, can have a high probability of profit.

For example, on February 6, 2003, the S&P 100 Index (OEX) was priced at 423. The following credit spread listed below had a *96%* probability of *not* hitting our set stop loss of *451,* thereby, making a profit of *$50* .

1. Sell OEX 460 call at 1

2. Buy OEX 470 call at .5

Credit price was .5 ($50).

Credit spreads do have risk—the distance between the strike prices of the option you sell and the option you buy. An OEX 460-470 credit spread has 10 points ($1000) of risk, less your credit. The wider the spread, the greater the risk.

To defend against the risk, you need to build in some safe-guards. First, you need to set a stop-loss. I always set my stop-loss out-of-the-money and away from the strike price of the option I am writing. If I am writing the OEX 400 call as part of the spread, I would set my stop-loss at about 395.

Second, I make sure there is a high probability that the index price will not hit the stop-loss. If the probability is greater than 20% of hitting the stop-loss during the life of the option, I pass. A simulator is used to measure the probability.

Third, I never buck the trend of the market. Never will I enter put spreads in the teeth of a decline.

Finally, make sure to take profits and close out your position if the spread narrows and generates a good profit during the life of the trade. In other words, get out of the hot seat as soon as possible. Also, exit if the market trend turns against you or if you get uncomfortable in the position.

98

RULES
OF THE ROAD
FOR INDEX
CREDIT
SPREADS

Here are the guidelines I have set for *index credit spreads*:

1. Use index options.
2. Sell (write) a far-out-of-the-money index option.
3. Buy an index option that is 5, 10, or 15 points further out-of-the-money.
4. Make certain to get a credit of at least .45.

5. Enter such spreads with less than three weeks before expiration.
6. Set a stop-loss that is out-of-the-money for the option you have written.
7. Set a stop-loss where there is an 85% chance of not touching the stop-loss.

Secret

99

THE RATIO HEDGE

The *ratio hedge* can be a high powered option strategy, but it involves naked writing, so it should only be used by option players who understand and can tolerate the high risks of naked writing. The hedging nature of this strategy reduces some of the risk, but you still face some unlimited risk.

In the 1970's, I was introduced to ratio hedging by a great classic book, *Beat the Market*, written by Edward Thorp, a math professor, a true pioneer. He beat the casinos and game of black-jack with a counting strategy revealed in his book, *Beat the Dealer*.

In his book, *Beat the Market*, he introduced a strategy where you purchased the underlying stock and sold short three overpriced warrants against the stock. Warrants are like long term options or Leaps®, so with Leaps® you can create similar strategies. Such strategies can develop some excellent risk-reward pictures.

The key to success here is to find some overpriced options. For example, on April 30 of 2001, Rambus (RMBS) was at 16 and the January 2003 25 call was 8. Buying the stock and selling two Jan 03 calls at 8 gives us 16 points in premium, offsetting all the risk of owning the stock. However, we are naked one option— above 25.

This strategy has a very wide profit range, from a Rambus price of 0–50. If Rambus is in that range at January 2003 expiration, you have a profit. Why? If Rambus is at 25, you have a profit of 9 points in the stock and of 16 points in option premium for a total of 25 points to cover your one naked option.

Consequently, only if Rambus were above 50 would you lose money. Maximum profits of $2500 occur if Rambus is at 25 at January expiration. Profits can develop during the life of this trade as the options you have written lose their value.

Not only can you design excellent strategies with long term options and the stock, you can replace the stock with another long term option and sometimes create an even better risk-reward picture. Here you have a ratio spread. Ratio spreads and hedging are covered in more detail in my book, *The Complete Option Player*.

You can test your trade by using a simulator to determine what is the probability of hitting the stop-loss point or points of the trade. In the Rambus example, the stop-loss point would be 50, and your probability of hitting 50 would have been 4%, so there is a 96% chance of breaking even or making a profit. Rambus closed on January 2003, expiration at 8.05, so your profit would have been $805.

100

THE DIAGONAL SPREAD

One of my favorite trades is the *diagonal spread*. A diagonal spread is a time or calendar spread. The diagonal spread that I love to design is a special credit time spread. Here you write the near term option that is out-of-the-money and buy an option further out in strike and time in a longer term option.

However, I only do trades where there is a credit. This is a riskier trade. You are again at risk for the distance between the strike prices less the credit, but when the option you have written expires, you still own the longer term option. Again, use a stop-loss to prevent moving into-the-money of the option you have written.

Let's take a theoretical example. In June, if XYZ stock price is 30, sell the July 35 call and buy the Oct 40 call. If you get a credit for doing this, you probably have a good play. Specifically, if the July 35 call is 1.5, and the Oct 40 call is 1, you get a credit of .5. Set a stop-loss at about 36. If XYZ stock does not hit 36 before expiration or exceed 35 at expiration, you pocket the .5 point credit, yet you still own the Oct 40 call as a kicker.

Therefore, you can win in two ways, first keeping the credit and second owning the longer term option. Use a simulator to make sure you have a low probability of hitting the stop-loss.

Finding such a trade is not as easy as it looks, but those gems are there if you take the time to search for them. Try to stay with 5 point spreads if possible and the further out timewise, the better for the option you are buying.

Let's take an actual example, Anheuser- Busch Companies (BUD) on September 26, 2002:

Buy BUD Jan 60 call at .6
Sell BUD Nov 55 call at .9

Stock price = 52.2   Spread Credit of .30
Stop at 56.1.   Value of Jan 60 call is .20 at November expiration
Total profit at November expiration = .30 + .20 = .50

With this example, if BUD does not hit 56.1 or exceed 55 at November expiration, you would capture the .30 credit. However, you still own the BUD Jan 60 call, which was priced at .2. Consequently, if you were to cash in at that time, you have a total gain of .5 ($50).

During 2002 I recommended 18 diagonal spreads. Fifteen were profitable, or 83%, and the three that were losses were small losses.

Here are the guidelines that were followed to create these diagonal spreads:

1. Sell or write an option where the strike price is about 3 to 5 points or further out-of-the-money.
2. Buy an option that expires 1 month or more after the option you have sold that has a strike price that is 2 1/2 to 5 points from the strike price that you sold.
3. Try to get a credit or, at the very least, a very small debit for the spread price.
4. Set a stop-loss that is slightly in-the-money of the option that you have sold (i.e. a 55 call would have a stop at 56).
5. Try to select a spread where the option you are writing has less than 2 months before expiration.
6. Exit the spread when the stop is hit or at the expiration of the option you wrote or if that option loses most of its value.
7. With this trade you get a free option, the option you bought initially, so you could hang on to it, if you wish, after the option you have sold expires.

Here are some additional diagonal spreads, recommended in September of 2002:

1. Date entered: September 19, 2002.
   Buy Bank of America (BAC) Nov 75 call   BAC is at 63.35
   Sell BAC Oct 70 call   Stop at 71

Spread credit of .25
Value of Nov 75 call at Oct expiration is 1
Total profit = 1.25 (1 + .25)
Position did not hit stop.

2. Date entered September 12, 2002
   Buy Duke Energy (DUK) Jan 27.5 call   Duke Energy is
                                                    at 22.54

   Sell DUK Oct 25. call   Stop at 26
   Spread credit of .05
   Value of Jan 27.5 call at Oct expiration is .5
   Total profit = .5 + .05 = .55
   Position did not hit stop.

In both cases the stock didn't hit the stop, so a profit was guaranteed because we had a credit or money in our pocket when we entered the trade. However, even if the stock hit its stop, you may still have a profit as the option you have purchased expands in value.

One advantage of these trades is that even if the stop-loss is hit, you may still have a profit in the position, especially if it is close to expiration of the option you have written.

Close out the whole spread at the expiration of the option you have written, unless that option loses most of its value, but use some common sense here. If the longer term option you hold has little value, hold on to it. Surprise volatility may give you a surprise payoff.

101

THE ULTIMATE POWER PLAY: THE SECRET SURROGATE

The best has been left for the last. One of the most powerful strategies that I use can create a powerful risk-reward picture. It is a *debit Leaps® spread* or long term option debit spread. This strategy can be used for stocks, indexes and futures. The more expensive nature of long term options allows you to create debit spreads that have wonderful potential payoffs, sometimes as high as 1000%.

And if you are fast on the trigger, on more volatile stocks and futures your probability of making a profit at some time during the life of the trade can be very high. This spread can also provide an excellent surrogate for stock or futures and can be a life saver if the underlying instrument goes the wrong way.

These debit spreads are a way of buying expensive options that are good value at lower prices. For example, on April 4, 2001, I entered a Cisco spread where I bought the Cisco Jan 03 17.5 call at 4 1/2 and sold the Cisco Jan 03 45 call at 1 for a spread price of 3.5 when Cisco was 13.7. The spread reduced the cost of the 17.5 call by 1 point yet only put a limit on my profits above 45. Altogether, I risked 3.5 (the most you can lose) to make a potential gain of 24.5, a 700% return if Cisco was above 45.

Here I had the chance of a home run, yet I reduced the cost of the Cisco 17.5 call by 22%. Also, using a simulator, I found there was a 80% chance the spread would double in value some time during the life of the option play.

And that is exactly what happened when Cisco rose to 24.You can't beat a strategy where you have an 80% chance of a 100% gain and a chance of a home run with a lower priced, limited risk trade.

Another example is a El Paso Corporation (EP) spread that I entered on September 23, 2002 when EP was 7.51. Here I :

1. Bought EP Jan 2004   5 call at 4
2. Sold EP Jan 2004   15 call at 1.9
3. Total cost and risk of 2.1

The position is 2.51 points in-the-money—more than the cost of the spread of 2.1. Your potential maximum profit is 7.9 points, about a 400% return if EP is above 15 at expiration in January 2004. Our simulator indicated that there was over an

80% chance that the spread would double in value. And again that is what happened when EP moved to 11.3.

When designing such a trade, the option that you sell to off-set the cost of the option you are buying should be several strike prices away. Try to design one that has a spread of 10 points or more between strike prices and shows a maximum profit of at least 400%.

Also, using a simulator, try to find one that has over an 80% chance of profiting. Take profits on half of your position if the spread price doubles in value. Let the rest ride for bigger gains but with a trailing stop.

The same kind of spread can be created with longer term futures options.

Why can you create such spreads? Because these are longer term options. The far-out-of-the-money options that you are writing will have a lot of premium, and the fact that you have a lot of time in these trades increases the chance of them paying off.

Again, such long term debit spreads make excellent surrogates for stocks. They give you excellent leverage with small downside risks. They are excellent for stocks where you are afraid of the downside.

Play some of the spreads on paper, learn how to design them, and you will have a powerful weapon in your arsenal.

CONCLUSION

These 101 secrets are the trading tactics, strategies and insights that I have discovered work in the real world! If you use some of these secrets as you develop skills to trade options, you will hopefully not pay a high tuition in this school of real life trading. You will make mistakes along the way, but these secrets should help you avoid the more painful mistakes.

If you have trouble understanding how to design some of these trades in the book, read my book, *The Complete Option Player*, which makes strategy design much easier and even includes worksheets to help with that design.

However, before I leave you, I have one last piece of advice to give you, and it is the theme of the whole book. Before you enter a trade, make sure you have an EDGE, an advantage over the rest of the crowd, whether that is an undervalued or overvalued option, a high probability of profit or a unique risk-reward picture. Make sure to have a statistical, mathematical or informational EDGE! This is the major secret to being a successful option trader. Also, be a maverick! Sell on rallies, buy on dips.

Section 11

Tutorial

What is the option game? It's an investment strategy that involves paying for the right to buy or sell stock or futures at a particular price over a given time, or selling the right to someone else to buy or sell stock or futures for a particular price over a given time. Simple? Actually, yes.

However, there is a bit of *pretending* going on. Most of the investors only *pretend* to want to buy or sell the stock they control. What they are really doing in this game is betting a particular stock or futures *price* will go up or go down.

That bet is called an *option*, and the casino palaces are *options exchanges*, the first constructed in the early 1970's. You can play the part of the tourist or the casino owner. Want to play?

Before you can learn the tricks of the trade, you have to know the game, and that is what this section is all about, teaching you the basics of option trading. (The good stuff comes later.) Let's begin.

Throughout the tutorial, we will use stocks to explain option trading, but keep in mind that what applies to stock and stock options applies to futures and futures options.

The Listed Option

The first step in becoming an effective option player is to gain a complete understanding of the focal point of the game— the *listed option*. A listed option is a stock option (remember, think futures, too), and an option is simply a contract, one that gives you the right to buy or sell 100 shares of stock at a specific price for a specific period of time. While stock options have been with us for a long time, the brilliant idea of creating a *listed* option opened up a whole new investment medium.

As a result, listed options are stock options that are liquid, standardized and continually created at the changing price levels of the common stock. When we say a listed option is *liquid*, we mean that it can be bought and sold at any time in an auction market similar to the New York Stock Exchange.

Formerly in the old over-the-counter (OTC) market, if you could find a seller, stock options could be purchased, but in order to have taken your profits from that option, you would have had to *exercise* the option, actually buying the 100 shares of the stock that you had the right to purchase. Now with the options exchanges this costly process of actually buying the stock or selling the stock is not necessary. All you have to do is go back to the Exchange and sell your option.

The Listed Call and Put

There are two types of listed options: the listed *call* option that gives you the right to buy stock and the listed *put* option that gives you the right to sell stock. When you purchase a *call*, you are betting that the underlying stock price will move up. When you purchase a *put*, you are betting that the underlying stock price will move down.

Parts of the Whole, the Listed Option

Using stock options, a listed option has four major segments:

I. The RIGHT—to buy or sell 100 shares of a specific stock
II. The EXPIRATION DATE—the date that your right ends or expires
III. The STRIKE PRICE—the price at which you can buy or sell
IV. The OPTION PRICE—the price you paid for the right to buy or sell 100 shares at an exercise (strike) price until an expiration date

This is an example of a listed call option:

IBM Jul 60 (at) 3

Let's look at each part.

Part I: "IBM"—This represents the stock name. This option is the right to buy 100 shares of IBM Corporation common stock.

Part II: "Jul"—This represents the time when your right expires. This is the *expiration date* which falls on the Saturday immediately following the third Friday of the expiration month. In this case, it is the month of July.

Part III: "60"—This represents the exercise price at which the IBM stock can be purchased. This price is also referred to as the *strike* price."

Part IV: "(at) 3"—This refers to the last transaction price at which this option was bought or sold with one qualifying point. The 3 represents $3, the price to buy one share of stock. All listed options carry the right to buy or sell 100 shares of stock. Therefore, always multiply the price by 100 to get the true price of the option. In this case, the true price is $300. ($3 x 100 = $300).

The Options Exchange

The venues for trading listed options are called the *options exchanges*. An options exchange, like a stock exchange, is an auction market where buyers and sellers gather to trade securities; in this case, the securities are listed options. The first of these exchanges, the Chicago Board Options Exchange (CBOE), was established in April of 1973. Because of its success, others have been established. They are our *casino palaces*.

(Again, remember when we say "stocks," we also are referring to futures.)

Options are also available on stock market indexes, such as the Dow Jones Industrial Average, S&P 500 Index and the S&P 100 Index, which includes 100 large capitalized stocks in its average.

The stocks that are listed on the option exchanges must meet a set of strict criteria.

Each individual stock must have at least three different options listed on the Exchange but can have many more. Each common stock has listed options that expire in the next two months, and every three months—up to nine months in the future.

In addition, in 1990, long term options were introduced. The long term options can run more than two years before they expire and are referred to as Leaps® (Long-Term Equity Anticipation Securities).

Why do some stocks have more options and more strike

prices than others? When options for a stock are first listed on the Exchange, options with one or two strike prices will become available. According to the rules, each will have four to eight listed options for a specific stock. If there is a significant change in the market price of the underlying common stock, new options with new strike prices then become available. Normally, options with new strike prices are established at 5-point intervals, unless the stock is below 50. Then strike prices are usually available at 2-1/2-point intervals. Many stocks have hundreds of different options available.

The Price of an Option

The price is the most important element of a listed option. The price of an option is set on the Options Exchange according to two different values: *intrinsic* and *time value*.

INTRINSIC VALUE

The *intrinsic value* is the *real* value of the option. This means that if you exercise your call option contract (which you normally never do in the options market), you will purchase 100 shares of the common stock at a lower price than the current market price of the common stock. Thus, the option has some real value.

If you were to exercise a put option contract with intrinsic value, you would sell 100 shares of stock at a higher price than the current market value of the common stock—the put option would then have real value.

TIME VALUE

Remember that an option is a right you have for a period of time. You must pay for that right, and the amount of money you must pay is referred to as *time value*, which is what the market thinks the intrinsic value of an option will be in the future.

As time passes, the value of an option will decrease. In fact, the time value of an option continually declines to "0" as time passes and the option reaches the end of its life.

The time value is the most important factor that we work with. In many cases, the options you buy will be options with time value only—no intrinsic value.

INTRINSIC VALUE + TIME VALUE = OPTION PRICE

Here two concepts should be explained: *in-the-money* and *out-of-the-money*. A call option is *in-the-money* when the *strike price*, the price at which you can buy the stock, is lower than the current market price. *Out-of-the-money* is, of course, the opposite; the strike price is higher than the current market price.

The option will probably be cheaper to buy when it is out-of-the-money, but buying the option, you are hoping that time will cure this and bring you in-the-money before your time (the option) is up.

An experienced player, whether he is a buyer or a writer (the seller of the option, the role of the casino owner), will spend most of his time with *out-of-the-money* options—options that only have time value.

To summarize, the option price is determined by adding intrinsic value to time value. Intrinsic value is the real value of the option. The time value is the value that you place on the possibility that the option will attain some intrinsic value by having the stock price move through the strike price and into-the-money.

VOLATILITY

An obvious truth—to achieve success in betting a stock will move up or down, you have to bet on stocks that are known to move up or down. Therefore, another element that controls the price of a listed option is the *price volatility* of the underlying common stock, the amount that the stock price moves up and down.

A common stock price that has high volatility normally moves in very wide ranges over a period of time. A volatile stock may move from 40% to 60% off its base price annually. Such wide price movements give it a much greater probability of moving through the strike price of a listed option, and, as a result, that option will take on more premium (time value).

On the other hand, a stock with low volatility normally trades within a narrow range, not moving very far in any one direction. This will have a negative effect on the option price because the probability of the stock price moving through the strike price is diminished.

However, understanding stock volatility in the options market can be tricky. In some cases, a common stock that has been historically quite volatile may reach periods in which it is somewhat dormant, and, conversely, stocks that are normally quite low in price volatility will suddenly move dramatically in one direction or another. These shifts in price behavior will alter the influence of this factor on the listed option.

LIQUIDITY

Though the price of the underlying stock, the time left in the life of an option, and the volatility of the underlying stock can be factors that constitute 90% of the price of the stock option, another factor that has a powerful indirect influence on option price behavior is the amount of *liquidity* that exists in a specific listed option. Liquidity refers to trading volume, or the ability to move in and out of an option position easily.

Liquidity requires that plenty of buyers and sellers be available to ensure such transactions. Options that do not have liquidity may trap you into a position or prevent you from taking a large enough position to make the transaction worthwhile. Liquidity in the options market can be measured by the number of specific listed options that are traded every day and the open interest; open interest means the number of contracts that have not been closed out and are presently open.

For example, how many IBM Jul 60 calls are traded on the average day? Calculating this average would give you an idea of this option's liquidity. Note that liquidity changes throughout the life of a specific option. The IBM Jul 60 call may have no liquidity at all when the stock is at 90 because the option is so far *in-the-money* that no one is interested in that option. On the other hand, it may not have any liquidity at all if the stock is at 30 because now the option is so far *out-of-the-money* that it hardly has any value at all.

Also, if there are eight months left in that IBM Jul 60 call, its price may be so high that it will lack the necessary liquidity to be an effective trading vehicle. In fact, options that usually have lives of seven, eight, or nine months normally do not have the liquidity that an option of two or three months would maintain.

Option Writers

If you are buying the right to sell or buy stock at a certain price over a given time, you have to be buying that right from someone. That *someone* is the *option writer*. In other words, if option buying is analogous to a side bet on the price action of a specific stock, the backer of that side bet is the option writer, the casino owner.

He takes the bets of the option buyer and, in a sense, pays off when the option buyer is a winner. When the option buyer is the loser, he pockets the option proceeds, what the buyer paid for the option.

Put simply, option writers sell an option rather than buy it. The option seller (writer) has a time advantage over the option buyer because unlike the buyer, *time* works for the seller. As time passes, the value of the option depreciates. This depreciation, this value, slips into the pocket of the option writer.

Let's take an example. Let's say that you purchase a call option—an Intel October 25 call. Let's say that there are three months left in the life of that option, and you pay a price of $300, plus commissions. At the same time that you are buying that option, someone unknown to you, on the other side of the Options Exchange is selling (writing) that option and is receiving your $300.

This money will go into his account, so, in a sense, you have just put $300 into the pocket of the option writer. Now he has certain obligations. If you request 100 shares of Intel by exercising your option, he must deliver to you 100 shares of Intel stock at a price of 25.

Let's assume that the Intel price is now at 23, which means we are working with an *out-of-the-money* option. One month passes, and the stock has moved from 23 to 24. The Intel Oct 25 has depreciated in value from $300 to $200, even though the stock has moved upward.

The option writer now has a paper profit of $100, less commissions. If he wishes, he can go back into the Options Exchange, buy that option back for $200, take his profits and, in a sense, close the casino door.

On the other hand, if he thinks that Intel is going to stay where it is or not move any further than 26 or 27 on the upside, he can hang onto that option and wait for it to continue to depreciate to zero. If you, the option buyer, hold onto the option, you will continue to see it depreciate in value, unless the stock moves up suddenly in a strong and positive direction.

In other words, the option writer has an advantage. While he is backing your bet, or option, it is depreciating. You, the option buyer, while holding that bet are losing money. However, if you prefer, you can be the option writer rather than the buyer.

That's right. You, too, can be an option writer. You can take the role of the casino or bookie. Where else can you do this legally?

Two Types of Option Writers

The *covered option writer* and the *uncovered (naked) writer* are the two types of option writers.

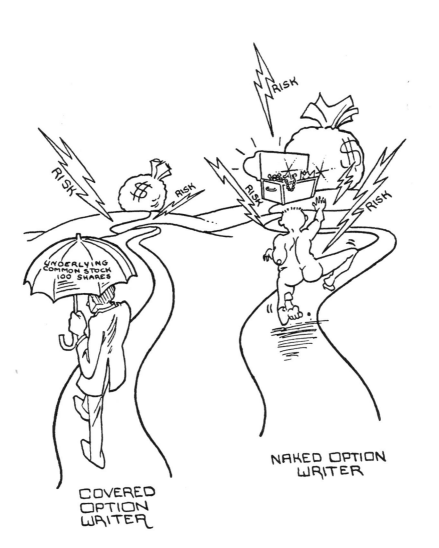

The *covered option writer* sells an option on 100 shares of stock that he has bought (owns). He benefits from selling the option, having the time value of the option on his side and, at the same time, profits from the upward move of the stock, offsetting any possible losses from the option he has just written. This kind of strategy is very conservative and the most popular today.

The *uncovered* (*naked*) *writer*, on the other hand, is very speculative and writes (sells) the option on 100 shares of stock that he does not own. There is unlimited risk to the naked *call* writer (betting the stock won't go up) and extensive risk to the naked *put* writer (betting the stock won't go down).

To guarantee to both the options buyer and to the Options Exchange that the naked writer will make good on the options that he writes, he must put up cash and/or collateral to back up his naked option writing position.

THE HOW-TO TO OPTION WRITING

The only difference between buying and writing options lies in the order in which you carry out the process. The option writer sells an option to open a position and buys an option to close that position. This process releases him from the responsibilities that are part of his option obligations. Conversely, the option buyer buys an option to open a position and sells an option to close the position, an act that relinquishes the rights that he purchased with that option.

The option writer, like the option buyer in the options market, has the advantage of liquidity. At one moment, he can write an option, and at the next moment, he can close out that position on the

Exchange by buying back the option. In this way, the shrewd option writer can avoid being assigned (exercised) by the option buyer or exposing himself to the potential dangers of option writing.

EXERCISE DEFINED

Here is where *exercise* should be more thoroughly explained. When you buy an option, whether it is a put or a call, you are buying a right to exercise. When we say *exercise* with regard to a call option, we mean to *call* from the writer (seller/backer) of the option the 100 shares of stock as specified in the option at the specified option strike price. The writer is required to deliver that 100 shares of the stock at specified strike price to the buyer if the option is exercised by the buyer.

With regard to a put option, we mean to *put* (sell) to the writer of the option the 100 shares of stock as specified in the option at the specified option strike price. The writer is required to buy that 100 shares of stock at the specified strike price from the option buyer if the option is exercised by the buyer. The writer who is being exercised is being *assigned* the obligation to deliver or buy the stock randomly by the Options Clearing Corporation. Therefore, the process of exercise is called *assignment*.

Spread Designer

THE DEBIT SPREAD

The *debit spread* is a way to buy an option at a lower price. The disadvantage is that you limit your profits. To design a limited risk debit spread, follow these steps:

1. Select an option you wish to buy, i.e. IBM Jan 70 call at 3.
2. Select an option you wish to sell in the same month but make sure it is out-of-the-money by 2.5, 5, 10 or more points, i.e. IBM Jan 75 call at 1.
3. Subtract the price of the option you have sold from the option you have bought, i.e. Jan 75 call at 1 from Jan 70 call at 3, and your total cost would be 2.
4. The result is the cost of the spread and your maximum risk.
5. The maximum gain can be measured by subtracting the cost of the spread from the maximum possible gain (which is the difference between the strike prices of the spread; i.e. 70–75 is a 5 point spread.) Using the IBM example, you will see that 75–70 is the spread, and the cost of the spread is 2, so the maximum gain is 3.
6. To evaluate a spread, you need to look at the maximum possible percent return and the probability of making a profit and making the maximum return. In our example, the maximum return for the IBM 70–75 spread would be 150% (300/200= 150%). A probability calculator can be used to measure your probability of achieving such returns. With the IBM spread, IBM must close above 75 at expiration to achieve a maximum return.

THE CREDIT SPREAD

The *credit spread* can be a way to write options with limited risk. There are two types of credit spreads, but all of them put cash or a credit in your account.

To design a basic credit spread, do and understand the following:

1. Select an option you wish to write, i.e. PFE Jan 40 call at 2.
2. Select an option further out-of-the-money to buy, i.e. PFE Jan 45 call at 1.
3. The difference between the two prices is the credit that you receive, i.e. $2 - 1 = 1$; credit of 1.
4. Your maximum risk is the difference between the strike prices, i.e. $45 - 40 = 5$; maximum risk is 5 points, less the credit you receive; $5 - 1 = 4$ points is your maximum risk.

ONWARD!

You now know the jargon and basics of option trading. If you keep the basics in mind, they will be a foundation for option trading success. How to build on that foundation, choosing between a myriad of trading strategies and tactics and picking those that suit your goals and personality, comes next. In this book the secrets of option trading will be revealed, and you will have in your hands the tools to build your dreams.

About the Author

Kenneth R. Trester is recognized as a leading international options advisor. He is a popular speaker at financial conventions and options trading seminars and has even given seminars in Russia. Through his market letters, he has originated many of the options strategies that are industry standards today.

Ken Trester is the author of *The Complete Option Player*, now in its 4th edition. It was followed by *The Option Players Advanced Guidebook*. Other works include a comprehensive options home study course, *Secrets to Stock Option Success*, and software for options trading, *Option Master®*, *The Push-Button Option Trader* and *The Push-Button Option Writer*. He has written numerous articles that have been quoted in such publications as *Barrons* and is a contributing author to the *Encyclopedia of Stock Market Techniques*. Ken Trester also coauthored the book, *Complete Business BASIC Programming*. Besides, Ken Trester is the editor of *The Put & Call Tactician* Advisory Service.

Ken Trester has been trading options since the options exchanges first opened in 1973. His background combines systems analysis, operations research and investment management. He has been the president of a management consulting firm and an Assistant Professor of Management at the California State University, Fresno and in the Computer Science Department at Golden West College. He holds a B.S. and M.B.A. from Utah State University and has done post graduate work at the University of Oregon.

Index

Please Send Me Information on the Following Products and Services:

Option Market Letter: _____ Put & Call Tactician

Books: _____ The Complete Option Player

_____ The Option Player's Advanced Guidebook

Option Software & Other Products: _____ Computer Software—Option Trading

_____ Options Home Study Course

_____ How to Buy Stock and Commodity Options—Video Tape

Option Seminars: _____ Option Trading Camps

_____ Option Trading Camp Videos

NAME _____

MAILING ADDRESS _____

CITY, STATE & ZIP CODE_____

Mail To:

Institute for Options Research, Inc.

P.O. Box 6629 Lake Tahoe, NV 89449

or call: 1-800-407-2422

Purchasers of THE COMPLETE OPTION PLAYER are eligible to receive a FREE copy of one issue of Kenneth R. Trester's Options Newsletter. To receive your FREE copy, simply fill in and mail this coupon.

NAME _____

MAILING ADDRESS _____

CITY, STATE & ZIP CODE_____

Return To:

Institute for Options Research, Inc.

P.O. Box 6629 Lake Tahoe, NV 89449

Internet: options-inc.com